GROWING AND LEARNING
Ideas for Teachers of Young Children

Jean M. Shaw

The University of Mississippi

Southern Association on Children Under Six

1990

Introduction

Educators today are concerned with quality early childhood education for all children. This resource book is planned for teachers of four- to six-year-old children. It presents a number of workable guidelines based on early childhood research and theory. It also suggests a wide variety of easily implemented activities to help children learn and develop cognitively, socially, creatively, personally, and physically.

Young children learn through active involvement and concrete experiences as well as through dialogue about these experiences. In this book teachers and caregivers will find descriptions of ways to involve children and to enhance their communication skills.

The book is divided into six chapters. Chapter One describes advantages of thematic unit planning and presents some samples of units planned around themes. Space precludes listing of all possible activities for the units. As educators read the unit plans, they can add ideas of their own and embellish the ones that are found in this book.

Effective unit plans are built around topics and skills from traditional subject matter areas: social learnings, language, mathematics, and sciences. Because these areas deserve special attention, Chapters Two-Five provide background information on the nature of each subject and implications for unit and curriculum planning. Each subject matter chapter includes several learning activities that educators may use in thematic units.

When early childhood professionals work together, share ideas, and generate new ideas together, they are more effective than they are when working alone. Parent involvement is essential for improving children's lives and learning. Thus, Chapter Six offers ideas for collaboration and for parent and community involvement.

My thanks to Sally S. Blake, who attractively illustrated the book, and to Julia McGehee, who edited the book and designed its format.

This book is dedicated to the Southern Association on Children Under Six staff, Board of Directors, and to my friends and colleagues in the Mississippi Association on Children Under Six.

Jean M. Shaw
Oxford, Mississippi

Table of Contents

Chapter 1

Thematic Curriculum Units

Most early childhood educators and caregivers are familiar with the idea of teaching through thematic units. In thematic curriculum units, most classroom experiences, projects and activities relate to a central idea or theme such as "Ourselves," "Spring Time," or "Dinosaurs." Work in a single thematic unit may extend from a few days to several weeks' time.

What We Know

Thematic curriculum units provide appropriate ways for early childhood educators and caregivers to organize educational experiences for four- to six-year-old children. In thematic units, children's knowledge, skills, and attitudes can all be developed.

Ideas and activities can be presented as part of an integrated whole rather than as isolated bits of information and disjointed things to do. Since young children acquire knowledge and skills in a global way, rather than in segmented parts, participating in thematic units suits the way children learn.

When teachers and caregivers use themes as a basis for planning, they can address many areas of growth for each child. Children's development in many areas--intellect and language, creativity, social, physical, and personal-emotional--can be enhanced. Since these areas are closely related, it is impossible to separate them effectively. With thematic unit planning, it is not necessary to do so.

Working with thematic curriculum units lets adults and children work with ideas comprehensively. There is time and room to pursue intriguing aspects of any given theme. When classroom work and play are organized in thematic units, both adults and children can be creative in their exploration of ideas and materials.

Because any classroom setting includes children with varying backgrounds, attitudes, and skill levels, learning activities must be planned so that each child can participate successfully. Thematic units offer opportunities for such flexible participation.

Guides for Classroom Practice

How does one plan thematic curriculum units for young children? How can units best be implemented? The following statements provide guidelines for planning and implementing thematic units with four- to six-year-old children.

Choose broad themes or topics to allow exploration of several concepts

Broad unit themes are easier to work with than narrowly-defined themes. For example, the unit theme "Ourselves" allows work with individual uniqueness in many areas such as physical abilities, feelings, appearances, and personal preferences. It also allows exploration of working and playing together in the classroom setting.

Get started in unit planning by brainstorming

Brainstorming ideas for a unit is best done by a group of colleagues, but the process can also be done individually. In the brainstorming process, many ideas are generated without an attempt to evaluate their merits. Once many ideas have been produced, participants then choose the ideas that seem most appealing and workable.

A first step in brainstorming might be the generation of six to 15 unit topics to use for a school year. Each topic that is chosen might be implemented for a period of a week to six to eight weeks.

Once unit topics or themes are selected, educators might brainstorm concepts or areas for study within each broad theme. One way to generate and record responses is to use a "web" diagram (Leigh, 1990). Educators could make a concept web, then also generate a web for experiences (projects, activities, trips, resource people, and other learning opportunities) to accompany each concept. Ideas can be gathered from many sources--state or agency curriculum guides, books, idea files--and can be adapted or created to fit the unit.

Based on educators' ideas, state or agency guides, and other sources, skills for children to develop can be "plugged in" to the design. Examples of a concept web and an experience web for the unit theme "Dinosaurs" follow.

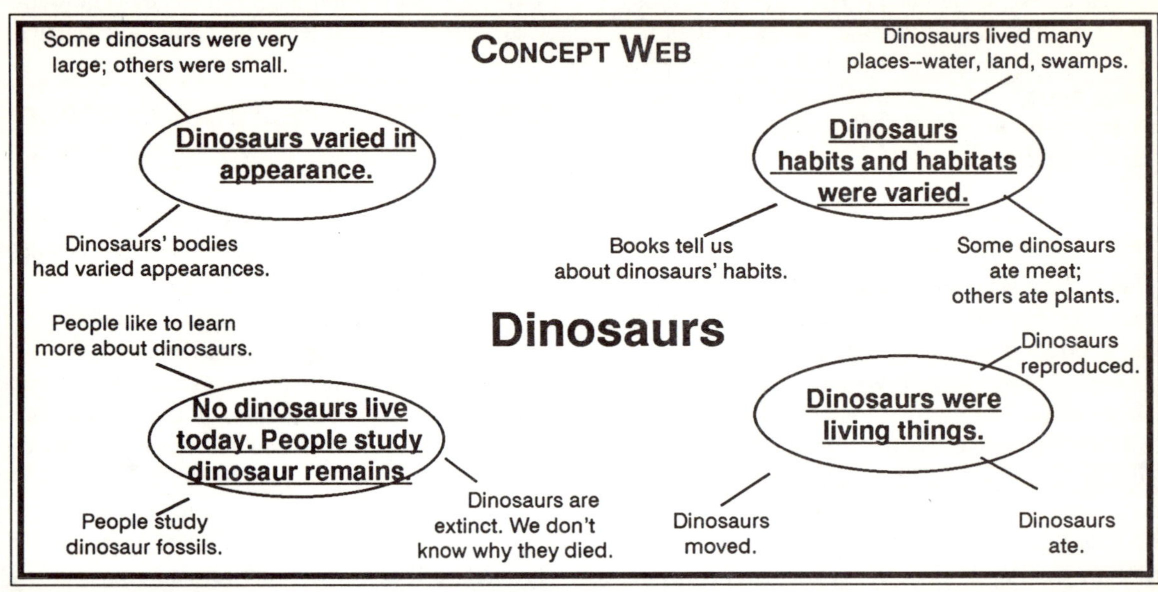

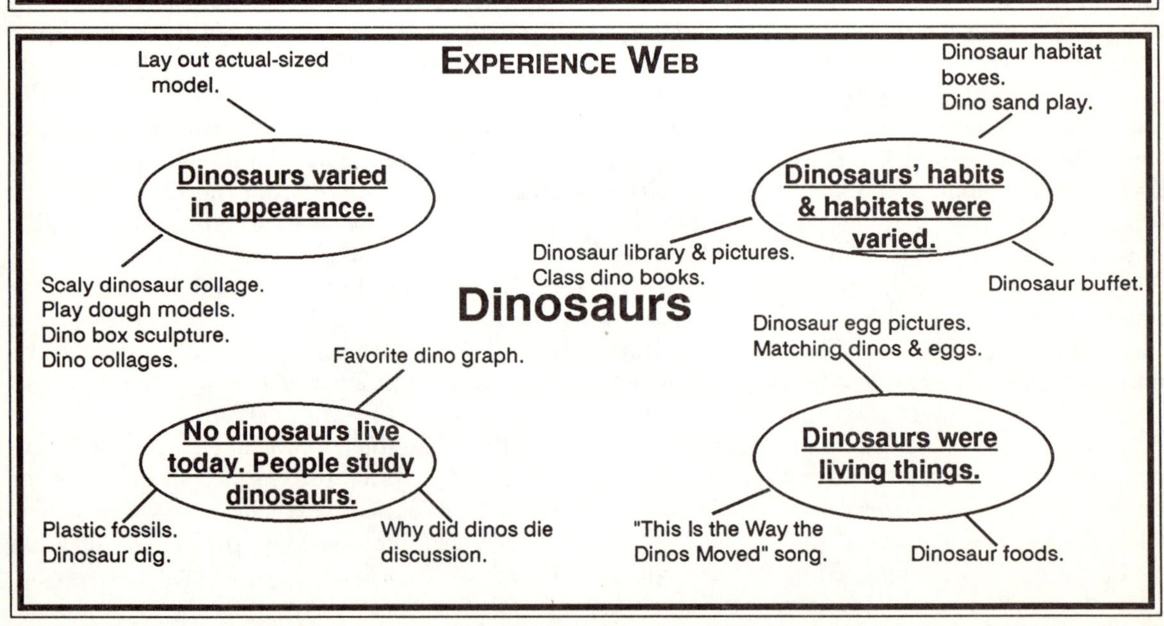

Gather materials and organize learning centers

Educators will want to examine the materials, supplies, and equipment they already have and decide how these resources can be used in thematic units. Blocks, water tables and materials for water play, games, dramatic play materials, art materials, and books and pictures hold potential for use in any thematic unit.

Teachers and caregivers may also want to add suitable props to their block, water or sand play, and outdoor centers to allow children to further explore unit themes. They will want to build art, math, and language activities around existing materials. They can plan to supplement activities and projects with books from the library, specially-ordered materials, and improvised equipment.

Children's families can also contribute simple materials to enhance units. Most families appreciate receiving lists of needed materials or possible contributions well ahead of the time the materials are needed. Requests for materials could be sent home in existing vehicles such a" calendars or newsletters. Letters, lists, and personal contacts are also ways to cultivate and enlist family understanding and assistance with materials.

Plan opportunities for children to use and extend their thinking skills

Opportunities for encouraging higher-level thinking in young children abound! As educators plan units, they should be aware of opportunities for challenging children's thinking. Creative thinking is important. It occurs as children offer many answers to open-ended questions.

For example, during an "Ourselves" unit, children can work in pairs. They can name many ways they are alike, then each pair can share an idea or two with the larger group. Children can then name many ways they are different.

Creative thinking also occurs as children are free to use materials in ways that are new to them. Children might use a stamp pad and make fingerprints. Each child could be encouraged to make a different, unique fingerprint design.

Questions like "How?"; "Why?"; or "What if?" encourage children to think on levels higher than simple recall. Translating ideas from one form to another challenges children.

"Tell me about the story in your own words." or "Let's show the pattern with other materials." are examples of requests that stimulate children to translate ideas.

"How can we solve this problem?" is also a useful question that can be used to stimulate higher-level thinking. Educators can encourage thinking skills every day, everywhere. With unit planning, integrating opportunities for extending children's thinking is easy and natural.

Leave flexibility in the basic unit plan to allow for children's ideas

Often children suggest valuable ideas that adults can follow up on and extend. For example, during an "Ourselves" unit, Carmelita brought some of her baby pictures to show her teacher. The teacher asked Carmelita to share her pictures with the other children. They discussed the many ways Carmelita had changed since her "baby days." The teacher encouraged other children to bring and share pictures. The teacher displayed some of the pictures on a bulletin board entitled "Who Is This?" Much examination of the pictures and informal discussion ensued.

Joey extended the unit further when he told about his baby brother. His teacher invited Joey's mother and brother to visit the class. Everyone enjoyed seeing and playing with the baby. Thus, the unit was enriched and extended by following up on the children's ideas.

As adults notice children's interest in particular parts of a thematic unit, they can also follow up on these interests. During a unit on dinosaurs, the teacher might help the children make and cut out a life-sized dinosaur model. The children might collage the model with pieces of paper to represent scales, thus giving an idea of a reptile's scaly coat. If this project intrigues the children, the teacher might capitalize on their interest by helping the children create a dinosaur's cave or eggs in life-sized or nearly life-sized models.

Plan to use local resources to supplement and enrich units

Local people, places, and things can be used in many creative ways to enhance children's learning. Children's family members can visit the classroom to "show and tell" special things. Local workers--mechanics, health care professionals, and hobbyists--can help to extend children's learning.

In most educational settings, resources are but "a walk away." In cities, children can observe plants and some animals in parks, empty lots, and along curb sides. In rural areas, children can gather natural specimens and observe various aspects of growing crops and caring for animals. In small towns, children can often walk to governmental buildings, businesses, and recreational areas.

For events to initiate or culminate units, educators can arrange for field trips to zoos, museums, and other special facilities.

Evaluate the children's work and behaviors throughout the unit

Many appropriate means of evaluation and assessment should be used to gather data on children's growth. During the course of a unit, teachers and caregivers might write brief notes concerning children's progress, interests, and behaviors. They might mark a checklist of behaviors as they observe the group of children at work.

Adults can collect samples of children's work to keep in files so that progress over a period of time might be studied and documented. Educators may also talk to children at intervals to see which activities they like and what ideas are being gained.

A teacher of six-year-old children might also begin an evaluative discussion with the entire group like this: "We've worked for two weeks in our unit on dinosaurs. What are some things we've learned so far? What helped you learn about the places dinosaurs lived?" The teacher might then ask the children to move to smaller groups and discuss the questions.

"When we studied kinds of dinosaurs, which activities did you like best? Why?" Group members can share parts of their answers with the entire class. The teacher might end the discussion by having children write about and illustrate some aspect of their learning. Discussions like this not only provide feedback for educators, but also help children reflect and summarize.

Evaluate the unit itself

Educators will want to make notes on their unit plans as the unit proceeds. Where adaptations are made, comments about the changes will help the unit proceed more smoothly the next time it is used. Children's suggestions can be noted for possible inclusion in subsequent uses of the unit.

At the end of a unit, teachers and caregivers will also want to look back and judge high points and things that were not particularly successful. Through constant adaptation and refinement of units, educators can best meet children's needs.

Educators must realize that work to develop a unit can pay dividends in the long run. Much time and effort goes into the planning and implementation of a successful unit for young children. However, units, especially ones that are added to and revised, can be used again and again with different groups of children. Thus, the initial work is worthwhile.

Many early childhood educators also find the work of developing and updating units very stimulating; it keeps educators "alive" professionally.

Ideas for Thematic Units

In the following sections are descriptions of learning experiences for the "Dinosaur" unit. Also included are samples of activities for "Ourselves," and "Springtime" thematic units. Space limitations in this book preclude listing every possible aspect or idea for units. Educators will want to adapt and extend the ideas presented here to fit their own needs, the needs of their children, and their local resources.

DINOSAURS VARIED IN APPEARANCE

From studying dinosaur fossils, scientists know that dinosaurs' sizes ranged from small to immense. A mussaurus ("mouse reptile") skeleton just 20 centimeters (8 inches) long has been found in Argentina. The codants, small, swift dinosaurs who ran on their hind legs, were only about 1 meter (3 feet) tall. Recently, in Colorado, scientists have unearthed bones of ultrasaurus, a creature about 17 meters (50 feet) tall.

Ultrasaurus would be three times as tall as a giraffe or as tall as eight or nine professional basketball players! Apatosaurus (once called Brontosaurus) was about 22 meters (75 feet) long and weighed 30 tons.

Dinosaurs' body coverings were dramatic too. Many had strong, scaly skins which served as protection. Others had bony plates which looked like armor. Many sea-going or sea-dwelling dinosaurs' bodies had adaptations that suited them well for swimming: streamlined bodies and webbed feet.

Scientists believe that some winged, flying creatures like Archaeopteryx had feathers; other flying and gliding dinosaurs probably had smooth leathery skin. As they examine pictures of dinosaurs, children will also be impressed by the dinosaurs' teeth, body proportions, and strange and distinctive shapes.

Scaly Dino Collage

Cut out a large dinosaur shape. Perhaps you could make a Triceratops or Stegosaurus. If you use several sheets of newspaper, you could make a half-sized (about 4m or 13 feet long) or quarter-sized (about 2m or 6 feet long) dinosaur. Provide newspaper and other scrap paper. Let children cut or tear lots of scales (it may take several days) and glue them to the dinosaur.

They can also add other details to the dinosaur--tccth, horns, bony platcs, and claws. Thcy can paint their scaly creature model if you wish. Display the model with a note that while it is large,

it is not life-sized.

How Big Was a Dinosaur?

Help children gain an idea of how very large some dinosaurs were. Work in a hallway or outdoors. Help children use a meter stick or a piece of rope marked in meters (or yards) and measure off a distance for a dinosaur's length or height. You might use one of these:

Stegosaurus--7-8 meters (8 yards)
Tyrannosaurus Rex--14 meters (15 yards)
Diplodocus--27 meters (30 yards)

Have some children stand at one end of the distance while others stand at the other end. Discuss the fact that no land animals today are as large as some of the huge dinosaurs were, but that some whales are that long.

Help children stretch yarn or rope along the length they have measured. Tape the yarn in place or "stake" it in place with tongue depressors. Help the children stretch yarn to give a rough outline of the dinosaur. Let the children walk all around it, noticing how large its tail, body, and head were. If possible leave your "model" for a few days, have the children help make a sign explaining what it is.

Grouping Dino Models

Display several plastic or rubber dinosaur models. Help a group of children describe the models and name some if they can. Ask the children to group the dinosaurs according to some characteristic.

For example, they could group the dinosaurs by whether they walked on two or four legs or flew, whether they have horns or not, whether they ate meat or plants, or whether they lived on land or in water. Ask children to suggest other means for classifying the dinosaurs and use their suggestions to make groups of the models.

Play Dough Dinosaurs

Display dinosaur pictures near a table where children can work with play dough. Encourage the children to make play dough dinosaurs and dinosaur eggs. Dinosaur cookie cutters may be used.

Toothpicks may be used for making dinosaur claws, horns, and teeth.

If any children want to dry and display their models, provide an area for them to do so. Play dough models can be displayed on styrofoam trays on which children draw background scenes.

Box Sculpture Dinosaur

As a "dinosaur favorite" emerges in your unit, help the children make a large model of it using boxes and other materials. Plan with the children the materials they will need (probably large and small boxes, garbage bags, glue or twist ties for fastening parts together, and paint).

Help the children solve problems of getting the model to stand on "legs" and supporting the neck. Help the children write and display a story about their box sculpture dinosaur.

Dino Collages

Furnish precut paper geometric shapes (rectangles, ovals, and triangles), plus scissors, glue, and background paper. Encourage children to use the shapes (and others they can cut) to make dinosaur-shaped collages. Ask them to describe details they have shown in their collages.

Dino Puzzles

Use posterboard and outline large dinosaur shapes. Cut each into several pieces to make a jigsaw puzzle. Let individuals or pairs of children put the puzzles together.

DINOSAURS' HABITS, HABITATS VARIED

Dinosaurs lived in a variety of habitats--in the sea, in coastlands, in swamps, and on land. Some swam; others flew or glided in the air; some moved slowly; others ran swiftly.

Scientists believe that many of the first ancestors of the dinosaurs lived in a warm period in which the world was dotted with deserts and with forests. These dinosaurs congregated around sources of water.

Later, dinosaurs also lived in warm climates in forests of pine, redwoods, and ferns. There were no flowering plants, but parts of the earth were wetter than during the earlier (Triassic) period.

Some dinosaurs ate meat. These creatures had to be cunning or quick enough to catch their prey. Their teeth and claws were long and sharp. Plant-eating dinosaurs had flatter teeth; many walked on four legs and were slower than the meat-eating dinosaurs.

Dino Library

Books tell us much about dinosaurs' habits and habitats. During the unit, supplement the classroom library with as many books as possible. Most dinosaur books are profusely illustrated; choose a variety of such books. Place a variety of pictures and posters around the classroom too. See if any of the children can lend pictures and books temporarily, too.

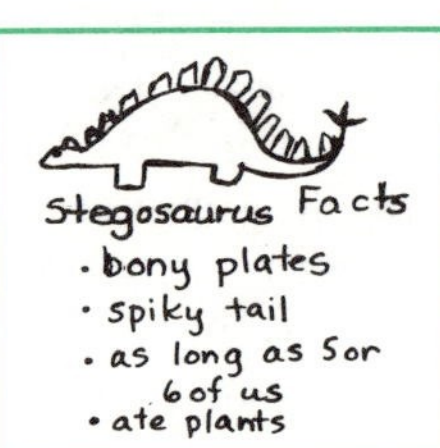

Dino Posters

Start a series of posters on dinosaurs to include in the unit of study. Write each dinosaur's name on the top of a poster board; draw or photocopy a small picture of each. Introduce each dinosaur; tell the children some facts about it. Read about each dinosaur. Ask the children to dictate some dinosaur facts and write them on the poster. Throughout the unit, as children learn more, add facts and observations to each poster.

Class Dinosaur Book

Make a class dinosaur book or several books. Ask each child to contribute at least one page. On the page the child might draw a dinosaur, then dictate or write with invented spelling some interesting data about the dinosaur.

Bind the pages together with staples, metal rings, yarn, or stitching. Place the book in the library for all to read. Titles that might be used for several books include **Meat Eating Dinosaurs, Plant Eating Dinosaurs, Dinosaurs that Lived on Land, Dinosaurs That Lived in the Sea,** and **Other Dinosaurs.**

Dinosaur Habitat Boxes

Use a large or small box to create a model of a dinosaur habitat. Help the children make trees and other plants from paper or gather greenery and twigs to place in the box. Help them draw water or place a plastic lid in the box and fill it with water. Children can draw other background details or use sand or dirt to complete their scenes.

Next, children should make play dough, oil-based clay, or paper dinosaurs to go in the boxes. Help the children write or dictate facts about their boxes. Display the writing along with the boxes. Encourage children to tell others about their box habitats, too.

Dinosaur Play at the Sand Table

Provide plastic and rubber dinosaur models to enhance play at the sand table. The educator can also post pictures of dinosaur scenes near the sand table. Let the children add pine branches or other foliage and "water holes" as they play with dinosaurs in the sand.

Dinosaur Buffet

After discussing facts about what dinosaurs ate, make a special "dinosaur buffet." Let children decorate butcher paper for a dinosaur tablecloth. Have a group help prepare veggie snacks such as carrot circles, celery sticks, squash rounds, and alfalfa sprouts.

Another group could help make tuna salad. Still another group might help to make and decorate dinosaur-shaped cookies.

Serve your buffet in courses. First, children can select plant foods--vegetables--and review facts about dinosaur plant eaters as they eat. They can next have their "meat course" and talk about meat-eating dinosaurs.

As children eat their cookies, they can review the fact that cookies are made from today's plant products--vegetable shortening, flour, sugar--and probably also contain an animal product--eggs.

After the buffet, write a group composition with the children. They could review and discuss some facts about what dinosaurs ate as well as tell about their preparations for the buffet and their reactions to it.

DINOSAURS WERE LIVING THINGS

People today know that long ago, dinosaurs were impressive and curious living things. They exhibited the same characteristics as living things today--they moved, ate, and reproduced. Dinosaurs lived millions and millions of years ago, long before people inhabited the earth. To help children explore the concept that dinosaurs were living things, the following activities might be used.

"This Is the Way the Dinos Moved"

Invite children to discuss and demonstrate the ways various animals move--some crawl, run, slither, and fly. Sing "This is the Way the Dinos Moved" to the tune of "This is the Way We Wash Our Clothes."

Substitute specific names of dinosaurs and let the children act out verses such as "This is the way Triceratops walked (heavily, with three fingers on head for horns)," "This is the way Pterodactylus flew (with gliding movements)" or "This is the way Tyrannosaurus hunted (menacingly with small forelegs held near chest and long fangs evident)."

Dinosaur Foods

Like people and animals today, different dinosaurs ate different foods. Some hunted and killed other dinosaurs and ate them for food (Tyrannosaurus Rex, Triceratops, Coelophysis). Other dinosaurs ate plants (Plateosaurus, Diplodocus, Apatosaurus).

Show children pictures of dinosaurs in which their eating habits are shown. As they find information on eating habits of dinosaurs, add it to a chart with sections for "Meat Eaters" and "Plant Eaters." Encourage children to draw pictures of each kind of dinosaur and add them to the chart.

Dinosaurs' Eggs

Scientists think that most dinosaurs were reptiles. Like modern reptiles, they reproduced by laying eggs. Scientists have found fossils of many kinds of dinosaur eggs.

Show children pictures of modern reptiles (turtles, lizards, alligators, crocodiles, snakes) and their eggs. Help children draw, color, and cut large egg-shaped (reptile eggs are round as well as oval like birds' eggs) pieces of paper. On the other side of their egg shapes, help children draw "baby dinosaurs"--creatures that will hatch from the eggs. Display the egg shapes taped on a window. Children will be able to see through the paper and see the baby dinosaurs inside their eggs.

Egg Match

Make paper dinosaur figures and large eggs. Write numerals or dot patterns on the eggs. Have children match the eggs and the appropriate numbers of dinosaurs. As children make sets of dinosaurs, ask "Count these for me." or "Which set has more or are they the same? How can you tell?"

NO DINOSAURS LIVE TODAY; PEOPLE STUDY DINOSAUR REMAINS

In the early 1800's, scientists and hobbyists began to study fossils and other dinosaur remains. Since this time, people have learned much about the fascinating creatures and plants that lived on our planet long ago. We do not know exactly why the dinosaurs died out or how long the process took.

Some scientists think that perhaps a star exploded close to our earth and its radiation killed the dinosaurs and many plants. Others believe that perhaps an asteroid hit our earth and exploded. Dust from the explosion kept sunlight from reaching the earth for many years. Without sunlight, most plants died. Thus, the plant-eating dinosaurs and the meat-eaters who preyed on them died.

Still other scientists think that the earth's weather may have turned very cold and the dinosaurs died from exposure. Some scholars also think that perhaps small mammals ate all the dinosaurs' eggs or perhaps diseases killed both the dinosaurs and ancient plants.

The extinction of dinosaurs may have occurred in a 100-year period or it may have taken a million years. Maybe no single cause killed the dinosaurs. The earth is always changing and perhaps dinosaurs could not adapt to changes quickly enough to survive.

Whatever the reasons dinosaurs died, people of all ages continue to be fascinated by them. Scientists (Paleontologists) unearth and study their fossils. Whole skeletons have been found and reassembled. Artists use these skeletons as well as their knowledge of today's animals to draw and paint vivid pictures of what dinosaurs probably looked like. People today can wonder at and try to learn more about dinosaurs.

Why Did the Dinosaurs Die?

The educator might want to present this question to the children as a mystery. Be sure to present each possible reason the dinosaurs died as a theory; scientists may never know definitively why the dinosaurs died. Invite the children's ideas on why dinosaurs became extinct, too.

Making Fossils

Fossils are made when dinosaur bones are pressed under layers of heavy material; the bones literally turn to stone. Fossils are also created when liquid material fills a hollow space such as a footprint and solidifies. Help children make dinosaur "fossils" with plaster of paris.

Use small plastic dinosaur models. Help the

children press the models into oil-based clay to make an imprint. Then, fill the imprint with plaster of paris (mixed at the last minute with water to thick cream consistency). When the plaster hardens (15-30 minutes), help the children carefully remove the clay and examine their "fossils."

Also, make footprint "fossils" outdoors. Find an area of mud or sand where there are animal footprints (dogs, cats, or birds may be easy to find). Or use a large plastic or rubber model and use it to make footprints in sand or mud. Pour small amounts of plaster into the footprints. Let it harden and carefully remove the plaster, perhaps digging around it with a spoon. Let the muddy plaster harden overnight, then have the children wash off the mud and examine their "fossil" footprints.

"Dinosaur" Digs

Bury clean, dry chicken bones in sand and let "classroom paleontologists" dig in with spoons and find the bones. They should "clean" the bones (perhaps brushing off the dust with a paint brush), then try to lay them out to reform part of the chicken's skeleton.

The caregiver can also bury small objects and pictures of objects that begin with the letters D-I- N-O-S-A-U-R. As children uncover them, they should name each object or picture and place it on a piece of paper marked with the appropriate letter.

Dinosaur Graph

One culminating event for the dinosaur unit might be a review of all the facts that the children have learned. Review your dinosaur posters and invite the children to help write a story about the unit.

Give the children square pieces of paper and ask them to draw their favorite dinosaurs. Have them tape or pin their pictures to a bulletin board, arranging the pictures in categories to form a graph. Help the children interpret the graph beginning with the question, "What are some things our graph tells us?"

SELECTED ACTIVITIES
FOR "OURSELVES" UNIT

A unit on "Ourselves" is perfect at the beginning of a school year. During the unit, adults can get to know children better and the children can learn about each other.

Educators might also plan the unit for the middle of the school year--perhaps when winter weather prevents regular outdoor activities. When the unit is used in the middle of the year, it may provide a chance for children and adults to get reacquainted and find out even more about each other. Following are samples of activities for the "Ourselves" unit.

Name Graphs

Make several name graphs over a week or more. Try these ideas. Provide letters printed on squares of paper. Help children choose the squares they need and glue them to paper. Use stamp pad letters and have children stamp the letters of their names in grids. Help children print the letters of their names on grids. Provide newspapers; help children select the letters they need and tape these to grids.

Once name graphs are made, compare the lengths of names. Help children read and discuss each others' names. Ask children to find other children whose names have the same number of letters as their own. Finally, use a name graph to play "Guess A Name," asking questions such as these: "This name has five letters. It ends in 'y.' It starts with 'J.' Whose name is it?" (Jerry)

"Favorites" Days

Plan a series of days on which children can

share some of their favorites. For example, you could have a "favorite colors" day on which children wear their favorite colors. On a "favorite toys" day, each child could bring and display a toy.

Let the children discuss and decide on a "favorite snack," then arrange to serve that snack on a subsequent day. On a "favorite animals" day, children could make masks and hats from paper bags to represent their animal choices.

A "favorite games" day could provide much unstructured time for children to play with their favorite classroom games. After several "favorites" days, educators could ask children for more suggestions, then follow up on feasible suggestions.

Baby and Grownup Visitors

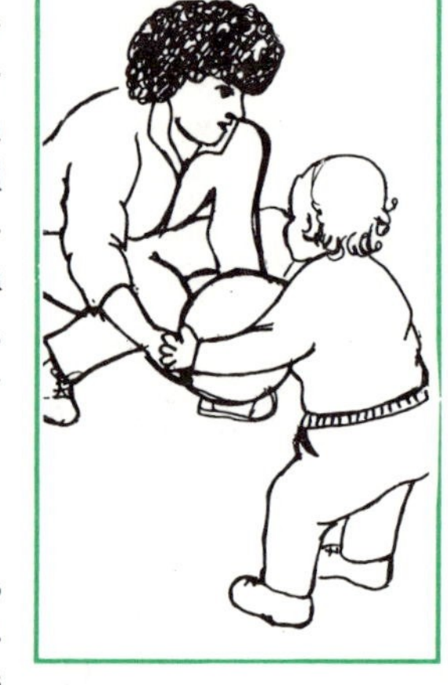

As living things, people grow and change. Make this idea more vivid to children. Invite a grownup to bring a baby to your classroom. Help the children get acquainted with the baby, talk to it, and see what things the baby can do. Discuss ways the baby is like the children and ways the children are larger, more independent, and more skillful than the baby. Ask the adult to tell some ways she cares for the baby. Help the children discuss things the adult can do and must do that the children cannot yet do.

After the guests have left, compose a thank you letter and let the children illustrate it. Let the children tell, draw, and write about things they did when they were babies, things they can do now, and things they will be able to do when they grow up.

"Gingerbread Man" Trip Around the School

People must work together and help each other in any educational setting. Help children meet and learn about the many people at their school. Read the story of "The Gingerbread Man" to the children. Arrange with various persons at your school to meet your class.

As you move around the school, write notes on gingerbread-like figures telling where you will go next. For example, you might show the children a gingerbread man figure that says, "Come to the director's office." After the children meet the school director, the director might say, "Here's a gingerbread lady figure. She says 'Come to the lunchroom next.'"

In the lunchroom, a food service worker might show the children the kitchen and tell them why their help is needed in keeping the lunchroom neat and orderly. After sev-

eral stops, return to the classroom and review with children all the things they have learned about the school.

"Loving and Caring" Books

Just as people need good food, rest, and exercise, loving and caring are important to our health. Talk to the children about the importance of loving and caring for others and feeling loved and cared for. Discuss ways people can be kind to others. Write their responses on hearts to display in the classroom.

Help children make books of things that represent loving and caring. The pages of the books could be rectangular or heart-shaped. One page could feature pictures of special people; another page could show ways to show others we value them. A third page could include cutout pictures of things that represent love. On a last page, each child could draw a happy face representing how he feels when he knows he is loved. Let the children share their books in your class library before sending them home.

ACTIVITIES SELECTED FROM "IT'S SPRINGTIME" UNIT

When the weather gets warmer, days get long, and spring flowers appear. Everyone's spirits rise. Exploring aspects of the season makes a wonderful unit for young children. The following activities are illustrative of the many that could be used in a "Springtime" unit.

Recording Weather Data

Enlarge the scope of the weather data you probably regularly collect. Have children notice and describe the clouds. Each day a few children could make a cloud picture by gluing cotton to blue or gray paper.

The children could make a simple rain gauge (simply placing a plastic container with a wide mouth outdoors) and examine any rain they catch in it. They could cut a strip of paper to the depth of the rainwater and tape the strip to a calendar.

Children could observe outdoors to see if the wind is blowing. Are leaves or tree branches moving? Does the wind make waves in puddles? Does the wind blow a flag or streamer?

Young weather observers could take turns being weather people and reporting to their classmates on a "TV show." They can talk into a cardboard "microphone" and tell about aspects of the weather while standing behind a box cut to look like a television screen.

Animal Visitors

Spring is a time of rebirth and new growth. Try to arrange for a visitor to show baby animals and give the children an opportunity to observe the animals up close.

Perhaps a farmer could show a young lamb or goat. A pet store owner might be asked to show baby rabbits or chickens. A parent could bring a young household pet for the children to see. The visitor could tell the children what care the animal babies need and what they will look like when they are grown.

After the visit, each child could draw a picture and the caregiver could compile a class book about the animal visitor. Help the children write a group composition letter of thanks to the guest.

Streamer Dances

In spring weather, it's fun for children to move outdoors for exercise and play. Provide 1-2 meter lengths (1-2 yards) of colored crepe paper for each child to run with and swirl through the air.

Challenge the children to move their streamers in circular patterns, in zigzag patterns, and in

different locations--above their heads, around their bodies, low to the ground, and so on. Use a tape recording and suggest that the children make their streamers dance to the tempo of the music. Dancing with streamers can be part of May Day festivities.

Real Easter Grass

Help children grow a beautiful bed of Easter grass for their eggs. Ask each child to bring a clean gallon milk jug. Help the children cut their jugs, leaving the handles intact. Provide permanent markers for them to decorate the jugs or punch holes along the top of the containers and show children how to stitch around the holes with yarn.

Help each child carefully place about 2 centimeters (1 inch) of potting soil in the bottom of the jug, then sprinkle on a liberal amount of rye grass seed. Remind the children to spray or water their grass each day; rye grass should sprout and grow in 7 to 10 days.

Springtime is perfect for an art show. Prior to the show, help children create special spring art. Tape pairs of pastel crayons together and let children scribble and color with these. Help children tape tissue paper petals and leaves to pipecleaner or wire stems to make large spring flowers.

Make string paintings and marble paintings in spring colors. (Children print onto paper with string laid in paint. They dip marbles into small amounts of paint, then roll the marbles onto paper laid in the bottom of a shallow box.) Save dyed egg shell bits and let children collage these onto paper. Help children create spring mobiles suspending pictures of spring flowers and animals from hangers.

Involve children in displaying artwork indoors and outdoors. Let the children color on paper to make a tablecloth or placemats for a refreshment table. Invite the children's families or another class to attend your art show and have some simple refreshments.

A Final Word

Thematic unit planning is very appropriate for meeting the needs and providing for the interests of young children. As educators plan units, they can take advantage of local resources while being creative in developing activities and sequences of events.

The possibilities for unit themes and activities are endless. The ideas presented in this chapter are just samples of things that educators can do as they provide high-quality, motivating learning experiences for children.

Chapter 2

Social Living for Young Children

Children build social relationships with other people almost from birth. Getting along with others is a vital skill and one that people use throughout their lives. Educators must encourage positive social relationships as they work with four- to six-year old children. With careful and creative curriculum planning, educators can also provide opportunities for children to explore different aspects of social studies.

History and geography are parts of the traditional social studies curriculum. Economics, psychology, and government are also areas of study in the social sciences. Even young children can explore aspects of these areas in meaningful ways. Social studies also concerns developing self-concept, learning about feelings, and developing attitudes of respect for self and others. These aspects are central to much that is taught and learned in early childhood education.

What We Know

Spokespersons for the National Council for the Social Studies (NCSS) in the document Essentials of the Social Studies (1981) assert that social studies education is vital to promote citizenship and to ensure the health of our democratic system. Effective social studies programs can help prepare people who can "identify, understand, and work to solve the problems that face our increasingly diverse nation and interdependent world."

NCSS recommends essentials for exemplary social science programs. Their recommendations include attention to the following categories: knowledge, democratic beliefs, thinking skills, participation skills, and civic action. Without facts, generalizations, and concepts, people lack knowledge for understanding of themselves and others.

Thus NCSS (1984) selected the following areas for developing knowledge: history, geography, government and law, economics, anthropology and sociology, psychology, humanities, and science (effects of natural and physical science on people).

NCSS defined democratic values and beliefs as a second category for social studies goals. Social studies education should not only present information about democratic values and beliefs, but such values and beliefs should also be modeled by teachers and reflected in the school's daily operation. Democratic beliefs are rooted in values such as justice, responsibility, freedom, diversity, equality, and human rights.

To help children connect knowledge and beliefs, thinking skills must be developed. The NCSS definition of thinking skills is broad and includes data-gathering skills, intellectual skills, decision-making skills, and interpersonal skills. Children should acquire information from different sources, organize and evaluate information, and communicate about information.

As children compare, classify, ask and answer questions, make conclusions, and make predictions, they use intellectual skills. Decision-making skills concern considering alternatives and their consequences, making and justifying decisions, and acting on decisions. Interpersonal skills include understanding of self and others, beginning to see things from others' points of view, working with others, accepting responsibility, and respecting the rights and property of others.

Participation skills and civic action are final concerns of NCSS for curriculum. As constructive civic participants, people use knowledge, beliefs, and skills in the classroom, home, and community.

To foster participation, social studies programs must help learners develop skills such as patience, perseverance, and working with others. Children must have opportunities for cross-cultural experiences. Successful social studies programs produce people who are willing and able to take part in public affairs in our diverse society.

Even such broad and lofty goals are natural to implement in the early childhood classroom. Ideas from the social studies help to bond together all the elements of early childhood curriculum. As educators help children converse, work together, and share, they build interpersonal skills as well as feelings of self-esteem and pride.

Cognitive skills such as classifying, comparing, and problem solving are inherent in most classroom activities. Children's concepts of communities and social relationships can be refined as they work together in the classroom, discover the roles of all the various workers in the school, and visit different places in the community.

Guides for Classroom Practice

To guide classroom learning, educators might use the following guides as they plan learning experiences for four- to six- year old children.

Model appropriate social behaviors

To teach kindness, respect, and caring, educators must model these behaviors as they work with children and other adults.

Balance curriculum with attention to different aspects of social studies

As they plan for young children, educators must give attention to development of knowledge, skills and attitudes. They should include activities that concentrate on different aspects of social studies--history, sociology, and economics for example.

Make cooperative learning activities important parts of classroom routines

Just as children are taught other skills and behaviors, they must be taught to work together. Doing things in small groups is natural for young children. Adults must make expectations clear: "When we work together, we share equipment. We exchange ideas and listen to each other. Everyone participates."

When children work together successfully, adults can recognize their accomplishments with specific comments and praise such as "Justin, you moved over politely so Cary could add to the design." or "I noticed that as you were working on the building everyone added ideas. You shared the work."

Utilize learning centers to promote social studies ideas

Charlesworth and Miller (1985) point out how well learning centers can enhance social studies skills, concepts, and ideas. For example, geographic concepts can be developed in the sand and water area as children build land forms, see how erosion takes place, and use transportation vehicles.

Also, children can explore different workers' roles as they model what people and machines do when digging, smoothing, hauling, and so on.

Take advantage of classroom routines to enhance social studies

Charlesworth and Miller (1985) also offer examples of how social studies themes may be taught through classroom routines. Time concepts, important for history, may be taught through use of calendars, timelines, and schedules. Basic ideas of economics can be explored as children need to use time wisely to leave time for special activities.

Decision making can be practiced in making choices of books, snacks, or surprises, then living with the decisions that have been made. Ideas of science and ecology can be explored, too.

Caring for living things develops concepts of interdependence. Appreciation for beauty and order can be heightened by creating attractive displays, keeping the classroom neat, turning off unneeded lights, and using supplies such as water and paper towels conservatively.

Use seasonal themes to explore social studies content

Through typical early childhood units such as "Harvest Time," "Winter Holidays in Other Lands," and "Warm Weather Fun," children can work with ideas such as change, similarities and differences, time, and family and community activities.

Involve children's families, community in classroom activities

Not only does the use of "outside people" strengthen the diversity of resources and expertise that educators can offer to children, it also helps to strengthen important home-school-community bonds.

Social Studies Activities for Young Children

The following examples of learning activities for four- to six- year old children incorporate some of the areas of concern expressed by the National Council for the Social Studies. Caregivers will want to extend the ideas and adapt them to meet the needs of their particular children. The activities described here might be worked into unit themes to follow the unit on "Ourselves" that is described in the first chapter of this book.

OURSELVES AND OUR FAMILIES. Educators should offer many opportunities for children to talk about and compare their families. Many different family structures are present in our society, and children need to know that all are acceptable. Whatever the structure, families have common characteristics--helping and supporting each other, living and eating together, and doing work and spending leisure time together.

Over a period of several days, the educator might help children talk about some of these aspects and make lists of things that the children's families do together. Educators should make sure that the classroom library includes books that represent different family structures and life styles.

Children might use tongue depressors or small paper bags to make simple puppets to represent family members. They can play with their puppets on little stages made from file folders or tissue boxes. They can use their puppets in small groups to "introduce" different family members to their classmates.

The children can use boxes, blocks, and other materials to make representations of their homes-- houses, apartments, trailers, condos, and so on. Each child could write his house or box number and attach it. The children might make graphs of their numbers of family members, places they live, or ways they help at home.

The children can make individual or group books about things they do with their families. Topics might include "What We Like To Do On Weekends," "Ways To Help At Home," or "Foods We Have At Our House."

The children might draw pictures for the books,

cut magazine pictures to represent their information, or dictate or write words to convey their information. They can create covers for the books, and the books can be placed in the class library area for reading. Individual books should be taken home eventually.

AWARENESS OF SELF IN A SOCIAL SETTING comes as children are oriented to both physical surroundings and social relationships in their schools and communities. However, to help them more fully understand their schools and communities, educators might help them look in-depth at facilities and people in these settings.

The children might tour one area of the school at a time; teachers should take time for the children to meet people and talk about their duties and facilities. At a school or community library, for example, children might see the work and storage areas. The librarian might show the children how she receives new books and how books are checked out.

Someone might read the children a story and let them check the book out for rereading in the classroom. The children might learn about some of the media equipment that is available.

Back in the classroom they might set up a "librarian's area" in the book area and play some of the roles about which they have learned. The teacher might help the children list all the ways the library and librarian help them.

The children might tour the school food service or a restaurant (in off hours). A food worker might show the children how meals and snacks are prepared in an attractive and healthful manner. He could discuss the ordering, transporting, and storage of food and the handling of money.

If several people work in the kitchen, the children might be able to see how they work together or how each does special jobs. If special safety precautions are taken, someone might discuss these with the children. To help the children internalize what they have learned educators can help the children set up a kitchen and eating area in the dramatic play area.

The children might also visit the custodian's area and learn how the custodial staff stores tools and cleaning products and how they work together to help keep the school clean and safe. A custodian might stress the need for each child to do her part in keeping the school clean, safe, and pleasant. The children will probably be interested in aspects such as waste disposal and light bulb changing.

After the children have made several visits, the teacher should talk with them about various workers they saw and the people that are served. Without many workers, a school or community could not run smoothly.

The children might make pictures or models of the things they saw. They can help to write thank you notes to the people they visited. The children might also make maps of the places they visited. Arranging blocks or boxes on a large piece of paper is a useful method for children to use as they begin map making.

DEMOCRATIC VALUES AND BELIEFS IN THE CLASSROOM. Exposure to democratic beliefs, rights, and responsibilities may begin at an early age. Young children can begin to learn about ideas such as people's right to security, equal opportunity, respect for others' rights, and honesty. The children can help to make the classroom rules. They can explore ideas on keeping the classroom safe. Their ideas could be posted on a "Safety Sally" snake cutout. As the children think of new ideas, these could be added to make the snake longer.

To encourage responsibility each child can be assigned special duties and privileges, such as being leader, helping with cleanup, and doing errands out of the classroom with an adult. Kindergarten children might also talk about their responsibilities as learners. The children can share ideas and experiences concerning their responsibilities at home.

Everyday happenings can lead to discussion of respect for each others' rights. "When someone speaks in a group, others should listen. What children put in their storage area should not be bothered by others. In certain games, we take turns."

Teachers can also read and tell stories in which honesty and caring for others is a theme. As children exhibit positive social behaviors, adults should praise them specifically and sincerely.

SOCIAL ACTION PROJECTS. Adults might help children plan and carry out a small project to help others. The children might suggest and talk over ideas, then vote and choose a workable idea. The voting process is simplified for young children by giving each child a small piece of paper or marker and asking the children to place their markers in boxes to represent the choices. If young children are asked to raise their hands to vote, many will raise their hands for each choice instead of only one.

The children might be able to carry out a project such as planting flowers in the schoolyard, visiting a retirement home, conducting an anti-litter campaign, or making a painting to brighten an area. Any of these would help others.

The children should plan the steps and materials they will need to carry out the project. If permission to complete the project is necessary, the children could help to compose a letter requesting permission. The children might plan with the teacher to divide into groups to work on the project. After the project is completed, the children should discuss and evaluate the results.

In a democratic society, people are free to express their opinions in responsible ways. Educators might help children write letters to legislators, school personnel, or community officials on issues that concern the children. Letters with suggestions or warranted commendations will be welcomed by leaders.

HISTORICAL HAPPENINGS. Caregivers might help children begin to develop a sense of history by thinking about events in order. The children might discuss what happens in a day or week at school. Each child might be asked to bring a baby picture and talk about things that he can now do that he could not do as a baby. The children might also speculate about things they will be able to do next month or next year.

Caregivers might also invite a senior citizen to visit with the children and talk about his early schooling and life long ago. If the visitor can bring pictures and artifacts to show the children, it may help them understand what the guest is describing. The caregiver can help the children compare and contrast what the visitor says to their own lives and schooling. The caregiver might help the children make a chart of similarities and differences.

At the end of each day or week, the caregiver might help the children recall some details and highlights. The caregiver can take some notes of things the children say. At the end of a month, the caregiver can help the children read and think

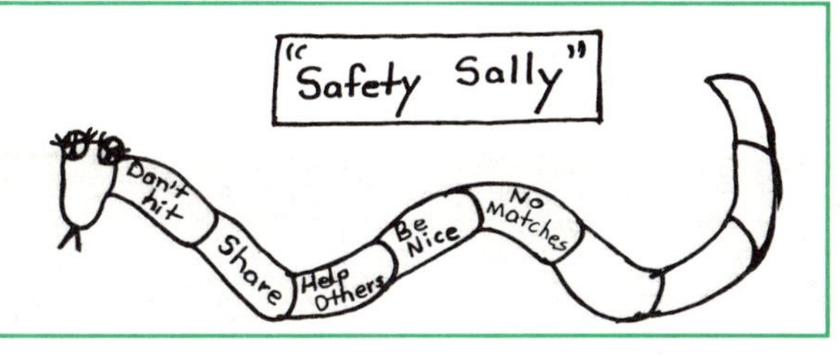

back over the month's events and choose some favorite activities or memorable moments. At the end of school year the caregiver and children could also review the notes again.

Such discussions help children recall and order events; adults can also gain insight into children's ideas of special events. Caregivers might share some of the things the children discuss with the children's families in informal conversations or in newsletters.

PLACES AND POSITIONS. Children gain a sense of geography through experiences beginning with familiar settings. As previously described, children might make a map or model of the classroom. Educators can help children add to and refine their maps by having them look closely at the classroom and see what details need to be shown on

the map. The children can discuss sizes and positions of objects in the room and try to show the relationships of these things on their maps.

Perhaps the art table is between the library area and the window; perhaps the table is larger than the easel, but lower than the easel. The children could try to show these features in their maps.

A teacher could take the children for a walk around the school yard and help the children notice and discuss various features such as hills, pathways, evidence of erosion, changes people have made in the environment, places where water flows, and things people have done to make the area safe and attractive.

The children could list some features they would like to show on a map or model. They could make their model outdoors, perhaps in the sand play area, trying to incorporate all the features they have listed. After initial work on the model is completed, the children might compare it to the actual surroundings and decide what they want to

add or change to make the model more complete.

SEASONAL CELEBRATIONS. Children can learn much about history, interpersonal relations, and the contributions of individuals and groups of people when educators use seasonal celebrations as unit themes. A favorite theme with much potential is "Thanksgiving."

Educators will want to begin by sharing facts about the reasons we have the holiday. They might use a flannel board story to convey the facts that long ago, in 1621, the Pilgrims of Plymouth, Massachusetts, were thankful for the help of the Wampanoag Indians and were grateful to Squanto, a Patuxet Indian, for sharing seeds and showing them how to grow plants and prepare foods. The English settlers were glad to have food for the winter.

About 50 colonists and 90 Indians came to the first Thanksgiving feast. Some of the colonist women and girls prepared the feast. The party lasted three days. The people ran races, paraded their soldiers, and played games. Some of the games they liked were wrestling, kick ball, and stool ball, a game like croquet. The Indians showed the colonists how to make popcorn and eat maple syrup on it.

Educators will want to emphasize to children that the Pilgrims and Indians of long ago lived differently than we do today. Their clothes were handmade and they had to make everything else they used. Of course, they had no electricity or telephones.

The Indians in Massachusetts lived in houses made of logs (not teepees). They protected the Pilgrims from other less friendly Indian tribes. The Indians taught the Pilgrims how to grow and use many foods--corn, berries, squash, pumpkins, apples, beans, and maple syrup.

If educators extend Thanksgiving study to include information about other kinds of Indians, they should stress that, for the most part, Indians were not savages and warriors. When they fought, it was to protect their land.

Indians in North America differed; their habits and lifestyles varied according to the places they lived and the resources they had available. Children need to be exposed to a variety of pictures of Indian clothing and dwellings. Educators might be able to gather and display real Indian artifacts--paintings, jewelry, pottery, baskets, rugs, and beadwork.

By becoming involved in activities and projects, children can learn more about the Indians' and Pilgrims' customs and lifestyles. Children can make simple costumes, sample foods like the ones the early settlers ate, and play Indian games.

For instance, they could play kick ball or hit a large ball through a coathanger hoop with a stick. The children can act out growing foods and preparing a big feast. They can make Indian cradle boards from cardboard and wrap dolls in the cradles.

The children might make "Pilgrims' boats" from styrofoam. They can try to shell an ear of corn and grind some corn between two bricks or large stones. Children can make coffee can drums and use them to create and "copycat" rhythms.

Caregivers can encourage children to feel good about themselves and others during the Thanksgiving season. They might let each child tell something good about himself and about a classmate. Children can write or dictate thank-you books for their families and decorate the covers of the books.

Children might write a group composition about things they are thankful for in the school, and share their thoughts with the director or principal, superintendent, or school board. Children might even write a congressperson or the President to express thanks for their school or the freedoms they enjoy in America.

Other seasonal themes might be built around winter, spring, or summer. In winter, educators could draw children's attention to changes in the weather--colder, shorter days will be evident even in areas where it does not freeze and snow.

Children might discuss special clothing they need for winter and dress felt dolls with appropriate clothing. They might sample foods associated with the season--hot chocolate or hot cider, for example.

They could explore the concept of freezing by placing water outdoors or in the freezer and seeing what happens to it. Caregivers could help small groups of six-year-old children read a thermometer. The children could prepare frozen foods such as fruit juice, ice cubes or frozen banana chunks. They would enjoy listening to stories about animals in winter.

During summer, thematic units can feature the study of water and leisure time activities. Lots of water play and play in the out of doors are appropriate. Outdoor time might be switched to early in the day when the weather is cooler. Children can design and experiment with boats. They can use magnet fishing poles and fish for paper or acetate fish cutouts that have paper clips attached.

Children will enjoy moving about an obstacle course "on foot" or "driving" cars made of boxes. Children can also discuss family activities during the summer. Parents will enjoy being invited to a picnic with foods prepared by the children.

CLASSROOM INVENTORY. Teachers can help children explore various economic concepts centered around a classroom inventory idea. The children can work in teams to count classroom materials in various categories--paper products, things made of wood, plastics, and other materials--or things used in the art center, block center, and so on. As they work, children use counting and classifying skills in a meaningful situation.

The teacher can help the children learn which supplies are free and which cost money. The children might help to plan some ways to conserve more expensive classroom resources. They might classify classroom materials as things they need to learn and "luxury" items. After examining some of the "goods" in their classroom, the children might discuss "services"--things people do to help each other learn and feel welcome in the classroom.

COMMUNITY HELPERS. Work with community helpers is an important part of the early childhood curriculum. Educators should help children explore a wide variety of helpers--traditional ones such as police and fire fighters as well as the many jobs represented by the children's family members.

In rural communities, educators will want to include much attention to various farm workers and their special duties. In cities, different types of workers from businesses and industries may need more attention.

Books and stories, visitors, and field trips provide ways for children to gather information about workers and helpers. As children gain information about various occupations, educators can help them assimilate the information by adding to pictures and charts; a continuing chart might include several kinds of community helpers to whom the children have been exposed.

The educator might write on the chart the children's ideas about how each worker helps others, where each works, and what special tools each

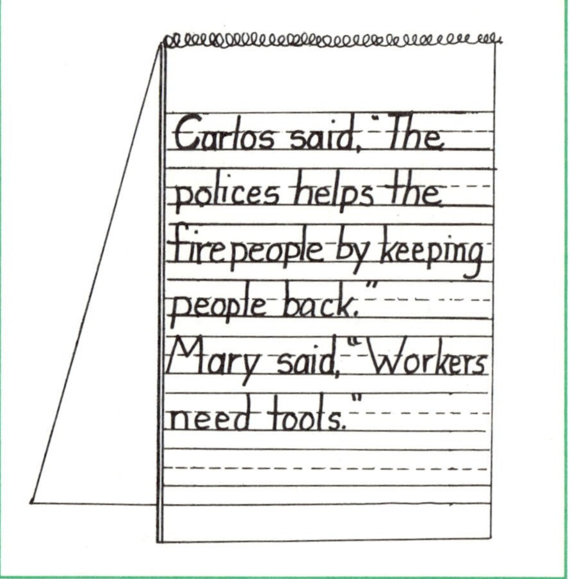

worker uses. The children might also note any special clothing the community helpers wear. Adults can help children make props such as hats to represent the various community helpers, and use the props in the dramatic play area.

The children might construct a large mural over a period of several weeks to portray the things they are learning about community helpers. Children can also make individual and class books about community helpers. For a culminating activity the children might help to transform the classroom into a community in which different groups of children have different jobs and offer different goods and services to others.

CHILDREN AROUND THE WORLD. Children can begin to understand that there are many children who live around the world. These children may live in different places and wear different types of clothing, but they share common characteristics with children in any classroom in the United States--needing care and support, living with families, and growing and learning.

Educators might set aside a special place in

the classroom to post pictures of children in other places. Newspapers and magazines offer a wide variety of compelling pictures that might be used. Educators could help small groups of children look at the pictures, describe what they see, and tell how they think the children in the pictures feel. Children can be invited to add to the display.

A class could correspond with children in another classroom. Teachers could contact colleagues in other communities or other countries and arrange for their classrooms to adopt each other. The children could send each other letters, pictures, or even audio- or videotapes. As the class prepares items to be sent to the other class, the children can help to prepare and address the envelope. Perhaps some children might accompany an educator to the school office or post office to mail the package.

Lokey and Leigh (1989) planned and implemented a project to promote awareness of our world community. The kindergarten children learned the song "One Light, One Sun" and sang it each day. They discussed the many children who live around the world.

The children drew pictures of children from different countries and cut them out. After the class talked about the different kinds of homes in which children live, the children drew pictures of homes around the world. The children thought of ways that people around the world can help each other and live in peace.

The teacher took dictation of the children's ideas, writing what they said on paper hearts. Finally, the children glued their pictures and hearts to a large round display to represent the globe. This literature-based project took several days; the children were able to express some of the ideas they learned as well as their own ideas as they completed the project.

Classroom Management to Show Democratic Social Values

As children and adults live together in the classroom there are countless opportunities for transmission of positive social values and behaviors. Management of time, materials, and interpersonal relationships are necessary for a smoothly running, comfortable classroom in which children feel secure, challenged, and where learning opportunities are enhanced.

Stress and tension are also lessened in a classroom where realistic schedules provide a framework for learning and growing. Teacher behaviors such as yelling, spanking, prejudice, and resentfulness send the wrong signals to children. If adults want to transmit values of fairness, patience, self-discipline, and reasonableness, they must practice these behaviors consistently themselves. If educators value independence, they must provide opportunities for children to make decisions and carry out activities by themselves. Educators must value and reward children's independent and creative thinking.

Prevention of behavior and learning problems is the best strategy. Educators can use several guidelines as they think about classroom management.

Strive for a busy, active classroom in which children are free to talk and move about.

Discipline problems are lessened in such a classroom. When children have many interesting, satisfying things to do and at which they may succeed, they are less likely to be frustrated, angry, and defiant than they are in a dull classroom with unrealistic expectations.

Young children are active. They are learning language each day and must be free to converse during much of the school day. They must have choices of intriguing things to do, but, also, must be expected to stay with and complete activities that they have chosen.

Plan activities for a variety of levels

Children in any classroom will be on a variety of levels and have a variety of interests. Therefore, educators must plan activities so that each child can be challenged and each child can succeed.

For example, as children work with clay, some will simply roll and pat the clay while others will be able to fashion realistic models. Both kinds of behavior should be acceptable. Pushing children results in frustration or compliance to please an adult.

If an educator plans a daily quiet time for children to select and look at books, children will need

access to a wide variety of books in different styles and on different topics. Some children will be ready to look at the pictures and talk to themselves about the books while others may be able to read some or all of their books.

If children are invited to draw and write about an experience, some will merely scribble and briefly discuss their products with an adult. Others will be able to write recognizable words using invented spelling. However, all children's efforts and progress should be recognized.

Develop cooperative behaviors in young children

Cooperation involves several pro-social behaviors such as sharing, waiting one's turn, helping others, and following directions. It requires children to work together toward a shared goal-- completing a project, participating in a smoothly running game, or having a pleasant conversation with lots of give and take.

Goffin and Tull (1988) express confidence in young children's abilities to work together, resolve problems together, and discuss interests and situations. They suggest that children be involved often in cooperative, rather than competitive, activities.

As children develop language and physical skills, they might work together to complete a mural. They might play "blanket ball" in which teams of six to eight children grasp the edges of a blanket, practice tossing and catching a beach ball, then pass the ball back and forth between teams.

Several children might work large-piece puzzles together. Each member of the class might contribute pages to a class book which one committee binds together; another committee could design the cover.

Help children gain self-regulation, control.

Glasser's reality therapy approach to discipline, described in Day (1988), is well-known. Glasser's seven-step method represents a positive way to help children assume responsibility for their own actions. The key to Glasser's approach is clear communication that each child is valued and respected. Children are not "bad;" only behaviors are.

The first of Glasser's seven steps is establishing communication with each child before confrontations occur. When inappropriate behaviors occur, children should be asked to assume responsibility; each child who is involved should be asked to describe what happened and to acknowledge responsibility for his or her part in it.

Adults should ask the children to discuss the effects of their actions and what the consequences were or could have been. The adult should then help the child to make a plan of how to handle the situation better the next time it occurs. The plan should be simple, easy to remember, realistic, and attainable.

Next, the adult should help the child make a commitment to the plan; the child should agree to stick to the plan. The adult should then help the child stick to the plan and praise positive behaviors and efforts to improve behavior.

Finally, the adult should accept no excuses for the child; the child should be accountable for sticking to the plan. Thus, children can learn to accept responsibility for and direct their own behaviors.

Make realistic, clear, high expectations for behavior

Educators must show and tell children what to do, then expect them to comply with expectations appropriate for their developmental levels.

Look for, change underlying causes of frequent misbehavior

If children are constantly restless at large group time, it may be that group time is too long or has become boring. Educators could shorten the sessions or find ways to make them more interesting by using puppets or other visual aids to hold the children's attention.

If children become tired and cranky most days before lunch time, educators might arrange for them to eat earlier, provide a midmorning snack, or plan soothing, appealing activities before lunch. If fights occur frequently out of doors, educators might plan for more supervision, a wider variety of activities, or ways to separate children before conflicts occur.

Manage different behaviors in different ways

Day (1988) describes Redl's suggestion that different kinds of behaviors and situations require different kinds of responses from educators. Permitting behaviors focus on what children can do rather than what they are not permitted to do. Educators should define expected behaviors, and convey to children appropriate times and conditions for the behaviors.

For example, children may run and shout outdoors, but not in the classroom. Tolerating behaviors means that under certain circumstances, behaviors that ordinarily would be considered unacceptable may be tolerated.

Redl describes three basic conditions for tolerating behaviors:

*"Learners' leeway," that is, mistakes in which children are learning new ideas and procedures rather than impulsively or deliberately misbehaving;

*developmental or age-typical behaviors that will naturally improve as children grow and mature;

*behaviors that are symptomatic of physical or emotional disorders and require constructive support and understanding from adults.

Educators must deal with some classroom behaviors directly. When behaviors are dangerous or cause chaos and disorder, educators must directly intervene and restrain children with words or actions. Children also need protection from psychological harm or too much excitement.

Consider children's needs as you plan and implement procedures for classroom management.

Morrison (1984) uses Maslow's hierarchy of needs to set the stage for classroom management to help children behave in positive, responsible ways. Some of Morrison's suggestions for happy, productive classrooms include attention to chil-

dren's physical needs.

When children are tired, hungry, and crowded, they cannot be expected to behave. Children also need safety and security; physical and psychological safety are important. Children need love and affection in the classroom to fulfill their need for belonging and affection.

Another area of need is that for self-esteem. When children view themselves as worthy, responsible, and competent, they tend to act that way. Views children hold of themselves come from their families and other adults. It is vital, therefore, that caregivers work to enhance children's self-concepts and help them experience success.

A final area of concern is that of self-actualization. Children want to use their talents and abilities to do things for themselves and to be independent. Teachers can help children be independent by helping them learn to make decisions, go to the restroom by themselves, and take care of their environments.

They can also help children set achievement and behavior goals. Statements such as "Tell me what you're going to do with the blocks." and "Let's talk about how you cleaned up the room." express confidence in children's abilities to think and act responsibly.

Social Living: A Curriculum Essential

Social studies provides a context in which children can learn more about themselves and others. It is a means by which people can begin to improve the quality of human relationships in the world. Social studies principles can guide educators as they plan for children and manage classrooms. What better investments can educators make in the future than to provide children with rich early experiences in social studies?

Chapter 3

Language Development in Young Children

Educators' interest in language development and literacy have increased dramatically since the 1970s in our country. New insights into the nature of young children's language and the ways that reading and writing skills can be developed are important in an information age.

Language is essential in communication as people express meanings and receive messages from each other. Early language concepts and skills are developed in homes and in day care centers.

Even four-year old children bring with them to school a wealth of communication skills and ideas about the uses and purposes of language. Educators can do much to extend each child's language bases in the classroom.

What We Know

Effective communication in our society is a blend of speaking, listening, writing, and reading skills. Humans want to communicate with each other. To communicate over time and space, people have developed formal patterns of writing and speaking. These are built on a foundation of oral language.

With time and appropriate experiences and support, children can become competent and enthusiastic communicators who can effectively use and enjoy spoken and written language.

Language development, like other areas of development, occurs in predictable, sequential stages. Social, physical, and sensory experiences are a basis for talking. Language is not learned strictly by imitation. Rather, Cazden (1981) describes language development as a creative process in which children assimilate and use a set of "rules" derived from what they hear others say.

Most adults have heard children say "foots" instead of "feet" or "goed" instead of "went." Children say these words not because they have not heard the correct terms, but because they overgeneralize rules for making plurals and past tenses. Language is also creative. As they learn to express themselves, children put words together in ways they have not necessarily heard or spoken before.

Adults can help children learn to use more words and phrases by listening and reacting to them. Leigh (1986) describes adults extending children's language by a process known as "scaffolding." As young children use words and phrases, adults attribute meaning and extend their beginning speech. Thus, children learn that language is meaningful and become more fluent in "adult language."

Cazden (1981) reminds educators that all through the language learning process, children pick adults that they know and trust to model. Even though children are exposed to standard English on television, they usually speak like their models--their families--using family dialects and grammatical constructions.

Children do not learn "correct" constructions just from being corrected. Rather, states Cazden, corrections must come from within; corrections and reinforcements alone do not change children's language patterns.

Like oral language, children's writing also proceeds in predictable stages. Children, calling scribbles writing, may make pages of continuous lines, zigzags, or circular marks. As children become aware of letters, their writing will include letter shapes, often the letters of the children's names.

Children begin to associate sounds and the letters they hear with "invented spelling." The first stage of this letter-sound awareness is usually the use of one letter to represent a word--"t" for "teddy," for example. Another important step is children's realization that vowels play a part in words. The word "teddy" may progress from "t" to "td", then to "tede" or "tedi" as children make progress in working with vowels.

After exposure to many books and other forms of writing, and after practice with invented spelling, children will eventually recognize and use conventional spellings of words. Researchers have shown that children who begin to write using invented spelling are likely to become better spellers than those who are taught spelling in traditional ways. (Templeton, 1986).

The relationship of storytelling to children's literacy development is well-established. Children who hear many stories develop a strong motivation for reading; they learn that reading can be very enjoyable.

Sometimes reading and telling stories takes place in a comfortable, comforting situation of physical closeness between adults and children; this contributes to child-adult bonding as well as building positive feelings about literature. Telling stories and reading aloud to children helps them develop the idea that reading and writing are sense-making activities instead of isolated activities involving worksheets, workbooks, and homework.

Moreover, hearing stories helps children develop language skills. Through stories children are introduced to the many ways that language is put together. They hear rhymes, alliterations, and new vocabulary words presented in meaningful contexts. Children who are read to also often become good listeners.

Listening to stories can develop thinking skills as children are exposed to cause and effect situations, sequences of events, and logical conclusions. Through stories, children begin to learn about and to appreciate the feelings of others. According to Trelease (1985), reading to children stimulates their interests and imaginations. Thus, there are many reasons to make storytelling and reading important parts of the early childhood curriculum.

Educators all over the world, concerned with finding better ways to teach reading and writing to children, have adapted their methods to what is called a "Whole Language" approach. Whole Language refers to a philosophy in which language acquisition is seen as a natural process in which children are largely self-motivated and self-directed. Whole Language in the classroom assists that process by building on what children already know, like, and want to achieve.

With Whole Language children are encouraged to read books and listen to stories that have particular appeal to them and to write stories and messages that have personal meaning. They are not asked to do many separate, isolated phonics or vocabulary exercises. Educators who use Whole Language don't think that children need a lot of rules and individual letters before they can learn to read and write.

Whole Language proponents are likely to use many "real life" materials and good stories with children rather than depending on workbooks and preprimers for their language arts programs. They plan opportunities for children to practice language in ways that it is used in everyday life. Children learn skills as they read and write, not before they read and write.

Guides for Classroom Practice

Language development takes place every day, in virtually every interaction in the classroom. To help them consciously plan for optimal opportunities for children, educators may want to consider the following guidelines.

Build on what the children already know

Educators must capitalize on the many things that children already know about reading, writing, listening, and speaking. They must build on the enthusiasm that children bring to the process of using and learning language. Educators must respect the language that children bring to school and use it as a base for language and literacy activities (International Reading Association, 1986).

Provide meaningful experiences around which to build meaningful language

Language skills and understandings are not taught effectively in isolation. Instead they must be taught in the context of rich experiences in which children are actively involved. Much natural conversation can flow from such situations; the situations can also be used as a basis for writing and for reading stories that the children have composed.

Be sure to communicate with each child

Research shows that adults tend to talk more to children who initiate conversation and who respond than to shyer, quieter children. However, these quieter children are often the ones who need individual attention and encouragement. Caregivers and their assistants should make talking to each child individually a priority each day.

Adults should try to ask open-ended questions rather than questions that can be answered with "yes" or "no" or a single word or phrase. Asking "Tell me about your new shoes." encourages a child to offer a more lengthy response than asking "Do you have new shoes?"

Use language in a variety of ways

Feeney, Christiansen, and Moravich (1987) outline some ways that oral language is used. Teachers familiar with these oral language areas can purposefully extend children's opportunities for using language in these ways. *Informative language* is used to share facts and opinions. Teachers can model this kind of language and encourage it in children. teachers should be respectful listeners so children know that their attempts to use informative language are taken seriously.

Descriptive language provides details. Adults can model this kind of language when they describe classroom events. For example, "La Shurn looks like she is enjoying herself at the easel. I see lots of red and green paint." Skillful teachers allow time for children to describe things.

Adults can help young children expand on their descriptive language. If Donnie says, "I did it!," an adult can expand on the child's language. "You finished helping to clean the gerbil cage. Now we can put in the fresh bedding." Adults should expand on children's language without being distracting or seeming to correct.

Another kind of language is *reasoning language.* It helps children understand relationships and solve problems. Adults can help children phrase and refine if-then type statements: "It's raining out. Let's wear our coats. Then we won't get wet." or "If you share the toys, then William will enjoy playing with you." Teachers can observe children's reasoning and problem-solving language as children work and play together.

The *language of imagination and recall* helps children talk about ideas of fantasy and things in the past. Teachers can help children who are unfamiliar with this use of language by recalling some of their own memories, asking children to recall events from the immediate past, and reading stories.

Language play occurs everyday as children invent silly words, repeat rhymes and chants, and experiment with language in other ways. Playing with language may help children think about language, so teachers will not want to discourage it. Using nonsense words, jokes, rhymes, and tongue twisters will foster language play.

Another type of language used by young children is *private speech.* Berk (1985) describes private speech as speech that is uttered aloud, but seems to be addressed to the speaker only or to no one in particular. Private speech seems to guide the learner; still at other times it seems to focus attention on solving problems. Early childhood classrooms should not be silent places. Private speech helps children and guides them.

Be a good model for communication

Teachers should show an interest in talking and listening. They should use language in a variety of contexts and for a variety of purposes. They should model a rich vocabulary and use their voices so convey different emotions. They should be likeable, respectful, affectionate models that children will want to emulate.

Be a good listener

Caregivers must model good listening habits. They should help children become better listeners by providing both structured and unstructured opportunities for listening. Brooks (1986) offers the following ideas for teachers who work with young children.

They can discuss and model characteristics of good listeners and reinforce children's good listening habits. Teachers can point out what to listen for. They should provide an atmosphere that is conducive to listening. They can encourage children to ask questions and make comments after listening experiences.

Encourage higher level thinking in children

Even young children are capable of creative thought, making conclusions, and analyzing material if they are asked to do so. Teachers must provide situations and ask questions to stimulate them to infer, synthesize, analyze, and evaluate rather than simply recall and restate information.

For example, after reading a story, an educator might ask "What would you have done?" "Why do you think...:" or "How would you make the story different?"

Use many kinds of literature

Educators should expose children to a wide variety of types of books and stories. They will want to use fanciful tales and more realistic ones, simple bibliographies, shorter and longer stories, books with and without words, and books with designs, photos and drawings as illustrations.

Educators will also want to share poetry with children. Poetry with its well-chosen language develops children's sensitivity to a different use of words. Young children will often enjoy the rhymed and humorous poetry of Shel Silverstein, Jack Prelutsky, John Ciardi, Dr. Seuss, and Edward Lear.

Use each classroom learning center as a place to develop language skills

Each classroom learning center holds possibilities for language development. Art work done by the children communicates ideas, but children can also discuss the processes they used to create it and the ideas they wanted to convey. Creations can be labeled with words or numerals by children or children may dictate things for adults to write.

During a "farm" unit children could draw, sculpt, and paint farm animals. They could "paint" and print with vegetable products and make seed collages.

The block center is a place rich in possibilities for oral communication. Educators may want to add pictures and props to the blocks to encourage children to extend their language further. During the farm unit, children might build farm buildings, roads, animal areas, and other structures. They might use rectangles of green and brown construction paper to represent fields and pastures.

When the children have completed special constructions, educators might take photos of the children and their products to serve as a record for future communication about what has happened in the block center.

The math and science centers offer opportunities for children to talk, record results, and use new vocabulary words. Children can use pictures, books, maps, and diagrams as sources of information. During the farm unit, children could grow seeds in dirt placed in foil-lined shoe box lids that represent fields. They could keep track of the growth of their plants with pictures and words.

They might also sort and classify animal pictures or models. Children could create seed patterns and extend, describe, and duplicate each other's patterns. Children could work with small containers of seeds. They could use a small scoop to take some seeds, then count the seeds and compare numbers with a neighbor.

Other centers offer possibilities for language learning. Activities that educators plan should encourage interaction, informal conversation about meaningful experiences, and use of new vocabulary pertinent to the unit. Whether children are working at the computer center, dramatic play area, or playing out of doors, educators need to be aware of opportunities for language growth.

Use group compositions to enhance learning

When children work together with an adult to write a story or list, they use a technique that is often known as group composition or the language experience approach (LEA). As they do so, children learn many things. They take part in the process of deciding on a topic and often on a title.

They observe that the adult usually starts writing at the top of the page and proceeds from right to left. They see correct spelling and punctuation modeled as the adult encourages each child to add to the story and writes down the words that are suggested. The children may propose and choose from several alternatives for the body of their composition. Often the children compose an ending.

With adult help, children can then read back over their composition. Since the focus of group composition is on creating and conveying meaning, writing becomes a true vehicle for communication. It transmits the idea that "We can write about things that are important to us. Then we can read what we have written."

Virtually anything in which the children are interested can become the topic for a group composition or LEA story. Some ideas include: "Our Nature Walk," "Our Favorite Things to Do at School," "What if People Had Wings?," or "Things That Are ___" (Choose a color, texture, or category such as things that are funny or things that are crisp.).

To sustain children's interest and participation in group compositions, educators can work with small groups so all children can participate and feel ownership of the compositions. They can encourage children to illustrate their finished stories or add collage materials to the pages. They can use children's names as often as possible in the stories and use different colors of markers for writing.

Emphasize writing; deemphasize handwriting

In the early childhood classroom, adults should place emphasis on the process of writing to convey meaning and not on letter formation and neatness. The latter approach is unsuitable for young children whose small muscle control is immature. When educators drill young children on handwriting and have them copy pages of letters, often children grow to dislike writing and are frustrated.

Graves (1983) describes five phases that are apparent in children's handwriting development. First is the "get it down" stage in which children make marks on paper with little apparent organization. Next is the stage of "first aesthetics" in which children become interested in attractive pages and do a lot of erasing.

Third is the "growing age of convention" where children want their writing to look conventional and become fussy about spacing, margins, and letter formation. In the fourth stage, "breaking conventions," children do not like to make a mess even though they know that editing and changing would improve their work.

The teacher's role is to help children recognize the need for drafts and editing. Graves' last stage is called "later aesthetics." In this stage children treat their first drafts as working copy that can be reworked.

Provide materials and experiences
to encourage progress in handwriting

Formal practice of handwriting is not appropriate for young children, yet adults can do much to help young children with the formidable task of learning to form letters and numerals. Leigh (1988) suggests some appropriate techniques to help young children.

Provide a wide variety of experiences with art, music (playing instruments), blockbuilding, and manipulatives (puzzles, nuts and bolts, puppets) to build fine motor control. Surround children with examples of print in a wide variety of forms.

Provide many writing tools: thick and thin markers, crayons, pencils, textured and smooth papers, chalk and slates, magic slates and so forth will appeal to children. Encourage children to use invented spelling and to "draw" letters as soon as they are ready (though all will not be ready at the same time). Provide models and instructions for those who want to know how to form letters.

Provide pattern cards for children to trace and cover with clay coils and "snakes." Encourage multisensory writing with materials such as clay tablets and templates, soapy washcloths, shaving cream-covered surfaces, or trays with a thin layer of sand or cornmeal in the bottom. Ask children to make labels for things in the classroom or things they have brought to school.

Help others support children's language development

Parents and other family members or community volunteers can be assets in the classroom. Children profit if more people are available to listen and talk to them, to take dictation, and to read to individuals and small groups.

Educators can assist classroom helpers in enhancing children's language growth by modeling and suggesting to volunteers ideas such as the following.

"Talk to children individually and in small groups."

"Be good listeners, maintaining eye contact, and offering nonverbal signs of attention such as nodding and smiling."

"Encourage children to extend their verbalizations by asking questions such as 'What else happened?', 'What else did you see?' or 'Tell me more about it.'"

"Help children talk into a tape recorder and listen to themselves."

Examples of Language Development Activities

Almost everything that occurs in the classroom provides opportunities for language development, but educators will want to plan and implement special activities to enhance children's language growth. On the following pages are examples of activities that let children use language in a variety of ways and contexts.

TALK, TALK, TALK. Oral language is the basis for children's reading and writing skills. Children must be encouraged to express themselves and listen as others speak. Educators must plan opportunities for children to talk and listen aside from the context of direct instruction.

Teachers might consider dividing children into groups of three to five for conversation. As children talk to each other, educators can circulate, listen in, and encourage. Educators might need to present and enforce a few simple rules for "polite conversation": Take turns. Be careful listeners.

Children might talk about topics such as these: "What did we learn today? What did we learn this week? What do you like about mealtimes at school? What are you looking forward to doing this weekend? How do you help at home?" After several minutes of small group conversation, group members might be asked to share some of their ideas with the entire class.

Children can use pictures as a stimulus for conversation. They might choose two pictures, perhaps from a grab bag, and tell about similarities and differences in the pictures. Talking about real objects is stimulating too. Educators can encourage children to use several senses as they observe: "What do the objects feel like? Do they have an odor? What sounds does an object make as it is tapped against the table?"

As resource people visit the classroom, children can listen to what they say and ask questions. Caregivers might help children prepare some questions before visitors arrive. After a short period of listening, the children can be encouraged to recall and retell some of the things the visitor said. Working in small groups, the children might talk about what they liked about the visitor or what they found interesting about the visitor.

As the class participates in special or everyday events, teachers can ask them to tell about experiences. Discussing an art project, a thunderstorm, a visit by the school's director, or a new book gives children a chance to express themselves, to sequence events, and to hear others use language in a natural way. It also gives educators an idea of what the children are learning and thinking.

STORYTELLING BY ADULTS. Reading to children is a familiar and valuable practice. Telling stories also has many benefits. The teller can maintain eye contact with listeners. Stories can be embellished or shortened to fit the audience. Storytelling allows for much creativity and imagining on both the part of the storyteller and the audience.

Telling stories using the voice and face alone to convey the message takes practice and artistry too. Props often give storytellers confidence and interest listeners. Cliatt and Shaw (1988) describe some props and techniques to enhance storytelling.

The storyteller might use a clothesline and hang pictures or small objects on the line as she proceeds. After the story is completed, the children might use the items and retell the story. They might reorder the items and produce some unique

changes in the story.

A teacher or parent might make a storytelling apron with pockets to hold small felt dolls or felt story characters. The characters can be placed on the apron or disappear back in the pockets as the story unfolds. Children will also love to don the apron and use the props to tell their own versions of the story.

Adults can draw story characters and background scenes on lightweight cardboard and then attach bits of magnetic tape to the characters. The characters can then be placed on a steel file cabinet, magnet board, or old steel cookie sheet. Again children will be attracted to using the magnet pieces to retell stories; they can also draw or select their own pictures to use as a basis for storytelling.

A prop basket or story box also helps a storyteller add suspense and drama as stories unfold. The storyteller simply collects objects and pictures to represent different aspects of the story, then takes them out of the box and shows them to the children as he narrates.

A brave and creative storyteller might even let a group of children collect props, then spin his story around the props that are available. Like other techniques and suggestions, the prop box or basket can be used by children to create or recall their own stories.

STORYTELLING BY CHILDREN. Children can extend and vary stories that have been told by adults. Creating their own stories is also challenging and productive. Children can use logical thinking as they sequence events and link cause and effect in their stories. Creating stories demands active participation. After children create stories, the stories can be written down, illustrated, and read by others. Thus, an exciting cycle of language usage is completed.

How can educators stimulate storytelling by children? Cliatt and Shaw (1988) offer some suggestions. Children might stand behind large cardboard cutouts and tell stories. Educators can cut holes in the cardboards for the children's faces to show through. Educators can prepare small figures or pictures and attach a paper clip to each one. The children can fish for the characters with a magnetic fishing pole, then tell a story with the characters they catch.

Educators can help children prepare a series of pictures to be attached to a long roll of paper and placed on rollers on a story viewing box. As they turn the rollers, the children can narrate the story.

Children can also help to prepare story cubes. On each face of a large die or cube, they can glue or draw pictures of characters. On another cube, they can glue pictures of locales or scenery. A child might roll the cubes twice to get characters for a story. Another child might then roll the setting, then the two can proceed to tell their story.

DRAWING TO COMMUNICATE. Drawing, talking about drawings, and writing are complementary language forms for young children. Educators can help children use these language forms often. Children might start out selecting a "background" picture, then drawing one or more figures to be cut out and glued to the background.

Adults can encourage children to talk about their drawings and take dictation of what the children say. Children who are ready to do so should be encouraged to write about their own pictures using invented spelling.

Children can use stamp pads and stamps to create pictures to use as a basis for conversation and writing. It is fun for children to make fingerprints from a stamp pad, embellish the fingerprints with features, then tell about these small unique creations.

Children might hold paper behind their backs and draw or write on the paper, then examine the funny results and discuss and write about the experience. They can also tear paper behind their backs into shapes, then name, add to, and describe the shapes.

The topics that educators might use to inspire drawings and extended communications are numerous. Some topics that children relate to are "Myself," "Things I Do at Home," "Our Classroom and School," "A Funny Monster," or "A Fancy Car."

Special holiday events and classroom visitors can serve as topics for drawing, talking, and writing. Children might also be inspired if educators take them to a "special" setting such as a porch during a rain storm, a shady breezy place on a hot day, or a darkened room to draw by candlelight.

CHILD-MADE BOOKS. To show that they value children's writing and to help children organize and share their writing, caregivers can help them bind pages together to create books. Books made by individuals over a period of time serve as records of children's thought and of their progress. The books can be used to gain insight into children's interests, uniquenesses, and modes of expression.

Books can be written by groups of children with volunteers contributing pages, or with each child asked to add at least one page. Once pages are bound together, books may be placed in the class library area, loaned to another class, or even checked out for overnight use. Books by individual children should eventually be returned to their authors to take home or placed in children's cumulative folders.

To fasten pages together, educators can use several different techniques. Soft covers can be placed over pages and stapled together. Pages can be hole punched and fastened to together with yarn, twist ties, or metal rings. Accordian-style books can be made by taping pages together. Topics for books can suggest unique shapes for pages.

For example, Jan wrote her story about a lovable snake on long snake-shaped pages. Ms. Enrico's class members wrote about teddy bears on bear-shaped pages. Tyrone's "Bright Ideas" book featured familiar light bulb shaped pages.

Teachers can make very durable books of the children's writing starting with contact-paper covered fronts and backs cut a little larger than the children's pages. The children pages can be stapled together, then fastened inside the covers with staples. rings, brads, or glue.

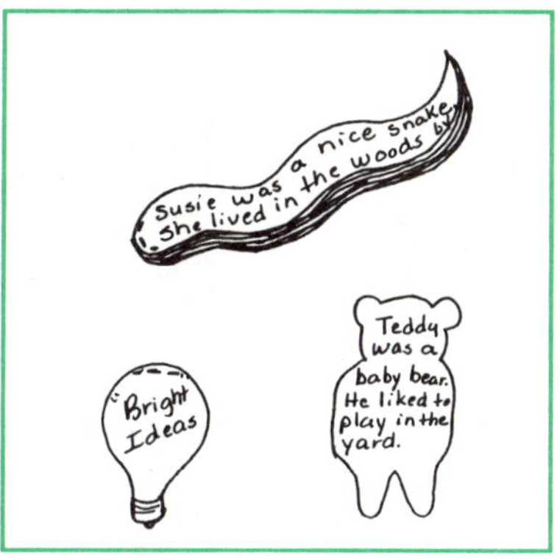

BIG BOOKS. Picture books of impressively large sizes are now marketed as "Big Books." These books are fun to use with larger groups of children; educators can be sure that all children can see the pictures. Small groups of children and individuals also like to lay big books out on the rug and pore through the pictures and retell the stories.

Children can work together and write and draw their own big books. The teacher might help a group of five or six children decide on a story. The children might phrase the story, then decide how to allocate a line or two of the story to each of several pages for their big book.

The teacher might print the lines along the bottoms of big pages. The children can then illustrate their pages. Teachers will need to encourage most children to make their drawings large enough for big book size. A child might create the cover for the group's big book and be sure to include each author's name on a title page. To make the book sturdy enough to be used, the covers should be made of cardboard or posterboard.

The children or teacher will want to read the big book to the class several times. Perhaps the authors of a big book could read it to another class. After the children are very familiar with the big book, children might vary its plot or ending, act out the story, or make a story map.

POETRY POTPOURRI. Educators will want to share poetry with children often. Poems can be read and recited during story time, as the children settle down to rest, or as the children are waiting for other activities. McClelland (1988) suggests that educators set up an inviting poetry corner in which books, children's poems, or posters with poems can be displayed.

To help the children become familiar with the way poems are printed and formatted, children need opportunities to see poems in print. Poetry books that are displayed should contain a variety of kinds of attractive illustrations.

A "poetree" can be used to display children illustrations of their favorite poems, lines of poetry they have chosen to copy, or follow-up art activities made after listening to poems. A poetree can be made from a bare branch supported in a can of plaster. Pictures and poems can be tied to the branch with colorful yarn. As the seasons and unit topics change, selections for the poetree can reflect these changes.

LISTEN AND LEARN. Listening skills are important and children should practice them in a variety of ways. Children should have quiet times and places to listen to music and tape-recorded stories. Children can also record their own voices and listen to the results.

A group of children might help the teacher carry a tape recorder around the school and tape familiar sounds. The other children could listen to the tape and try to identify the sounds.

The teacher might assemble a variety of familiar objects that make sounds (bells, a small drum, wooden blocks, pieces of sand paper, a few pennies in a jar). The teacher could hide the objects in a box, then use them to make sounds and ask the children to try to identify the sounds. The teacher could make sounds and ask the children to count the sounds; he could produce two sounds and ask the children to tell whether the sounds are alike or different. 

Adults can ask children to play a variety of games that demand careful listening. Before using listening games, educators should alert children to the fact that they need to be careful listeners because the directions will not be repeated. Most listening games should be played for only short periods of time.

For instance, an adult might ask children to listen and raise their hands every time they hear the word "the." If the children master this kind of exercise, they might then raise their hands when they hear "the" and stand as they hear "and."

Playing "Simon Says" is a listening game. Educators might vary it by asking children to respond to directions given in a high voice, but not respond to directions given in a low voice.

Following directions games may be simple or complex depending on children's needs. One child can be asked to follow directions. A second child can be asked to repeat the directions for a third child to follow.

Directions might be "Jose, clap your hands three times. Girls, stand up and reach as high as you can. Kelly, pretend to throw something in the wastebasket, then come back to the group. Boys, wiggle your feet, then give us a great big smile."

Brooks (1986) suggests several listening games that can be played with large or small groups of children. "Silly Sentences" involves listening for details. Children can stand when they hear a silly sentence and remain seated when they hear a sensible one.

A caregiver might use sentences such as these; "The bus driver bought gas for our airplane." "The chair hopped across the floor." or "The sun shone brightly yesterday."

"Which One Is It?" involves children in listening carefully to two possible answers, then choosing the correct one. A teacher might ask, "Which grows on birds--feathers or sweaters?" or "Which do we wear--socks or blocks?"

"Color Rhyme Time" is in a sentence completion format. Children can take turns saying color words to finish rhymes or each can choose and show a crayon or colored tile for the answer.

A teacher could ask the children to complete rhymes such as these. "I got a new bed and it was ___ (red)." "So fresh and clean, the leaves are ___ (green)." "Look at the clown. He's dressed in ___ (brown)." "Finish the Rhyme" is a similiar game except children use any rhyming word to complete sentences such as "I saw a bug run under the __." or "A big spotted frog sat on a ___."

Children can also take turns creating and finishing short ministories. They use inferential listening skills as they complete stories and answer questions such as the following: "Kethrick went to school. He left his raincoat at home even though his grandma said it might rain. On the way home Kethrick got very wet. He should have..." or "Samantha likes to bake cookies. She and her dad are very careful to measure the ingredients and mix them well. The cookies they bake..."

POSITIONS AND TIME. To enhance children's abilities to understand and use spatial and temporal words, a caregiver might organize a special scavenger hunt. Clues for the hunt should provide directions for finding an intriguing object. For example, the caregiver might hide a new book, a special picture of interest in the current unit, or invitations to a parents' night meeting.

The caregiver can hide the clues in various locations--high and low places, over and under objects, around corners, and between things. The caregiver can give the children the first clue and help them read it. They can then follow the direc-

tions and find the next clue, proceeding until the "prize" is found.

After they find the object, the children can gather and write a group composition about the scavenger hunt. As they contribute ideas to the story, the caregiver can help the children recall events and locations in order and use positional words such as over, between, and through.

The group can read back over their story and the caregiver can use a marker to highlight positional words. The children can review the order of events using words such as first, next, finally, and last. Children can reenact parts of the scavenger hunt illustrating the positional words they used.

BRAINSTORMING. Brainstorming is a process that challenges children and adults to use creative thinking. The process involves working together to generate as many responses as possible to an open-ended question or problem. In the first stage of brainstorming the focus is on thinking of many ideas, not on evaluating, refining, or elaborating on them.

A large or small group of children can brainstorm with an adult. After introducing the topic, the adult should write down the children's ideas as quickly as possible. When the children "get stuck," the adult can encourage the children to think of more ideas or the adult may suggest a new category of responses.

As Ms. Liang's group was brainstorming a list of things that are red, several of the children named items of clothing. Next, a child suggested "tomatoes" and others added "radishes" and "apples." Then no one could think of another red item, so Ms. Liang said, "We've named some red clothing and some foods...let's see...how about some toys or vehicles that are red." Her encouragement and suggestion, and perhaps the time for children to think, prompted the children to make many more responses.

After the group suggests some responses, the adult can help them read over the list; children may think of other items to suggest. The adult can then have the group categorize their responses; for the question "What is red?", categories of answers might be clothing, foods, classroom supplies, vehicles, items in pictures, and so on.

The adult can then help the children to elaborate on their responses. For example, Ms. Liang asked Vicki to tell more about the motorcycle she mentioned. Vicki gave an animated description of her older brother's "shiny brand new Honda motorcycle...red and shiny like fingernail polish."

Adults might also ask children to think of original responses--"Something really different...

something no one else would think of." Thus, in the brainstorming process, adults can ask children to use four interrelated aspects of creative thought as suggested by Torrance (1972). The aspects are *fluency* (producing many responses), *flexibility* (working with different categories of responses), *originality* (generating unusual responses), and *elaboration* (providing details).

Topics that children can use for brainstorming are almost limitless. Adults themselves can brainstorm lists of topics for children to use. A few suggestions follow: "Things That Are Smooth," "A Spring Day Reminds Me of ...," "Things to Do on a Rainy Day," "Ways People Can Help Each Other," and "Things That Come in Pairs."

JOURNALS IN THE KINDERGARTEN. Many five- and six-year old children can write regularly in booklets that serve as journals. At the end of each day at school for example, kindergartners can record in their journals things they did during the day.

They might focus on the thing they liked the best, something they learned, or some impressions of a visitor or science investigation. As the children work, the teacher might write notes in the journals of a child or two recording some positive impressions of things the child accomplished during the day.

Every few weeks the children can take their journals home and explain and discuss the entries with family members. Parents could add notes to journals, too, making them a viable and important means of communication.

Some teachers prefer to have journal writing time at the beginning of the day. At this time the children are fresh and can express some of the things that happened the previous evening or in the early morning. Some teachers wait until the second half of the kindergarten year before introducing journal writing.

Tatum (1988) suggests that journal writing should be a chance for children to express their thoughts and feelings. As some children write and draw in their journals, the teacher might take dictation for others, or add "teacher writing" (conventional spellings and punctuation) to the journals of children who request it.

Such a period of one-to-one interaction allows the teacher to individualize and to better understand the thought processes that are behind each child's communicative attempts. It gives the teacher valuable feedback about things that are occurring in the classroom.

Materials for journal writing should be stored in an easily accessible place. Writing materials and extra papers should be available to all children at journal writing time as well as at other times during the day.

Language Development: Every Day, Everywhere

Using language to communicate is a human activity. It is useful and can be a source of lifelong pleasure. Language broadens horizons. It lets people share facts, ideas, opinions, and feelings. It makes interaction possible across time and space. Language complements thought and is a vehicle by which people clarify and extend ideas.

Children want to communicate. When adults appreciate their communications skills and build upon each child's background, each child's growth and self-concept can be enhanced. Through a wide variety of informal and formal activities, educators can help each child grow in the use of language.

Chapter 4

Mathematics for Young Children

Mathematics is a vital area for young children to explore and learn about. Without mathematics we could not tell our ages, make comparisons in quantities, or think about buying things.

Young children enter the world of mathematics eagerly. They are anxious to work with numbers, shapes, and classifying. Work in mathematics is fun and challenging for youngsters; they do not see it as hard or something that is "mostly for boys."

When adults think about mathematics, work with numbers comes to mind first. A math curriculum for young children does include numbers, but it must also be built on important skills such as classifying, comparing, ordering, and patterning. The curriculum must also include work with geometry, graphs, measurement, and problem solving.

What We Know

The National Council of Teachers of Mathematics has published a document, **Curriculum and Evaluation Standards for School Mathematics (1989)**. This document provides guidelines for mathematics teaching and learning for the 1990's. The document includes guidelines for Grades K-4, 5-8, and 9-12 as well as guidelines for evaluation.

Stressing active learner participation, problem solving and reasoning, and communication in mathematics, the K-4 recommendations include attention to assumptions familiar to early childhood educators.

Some of these assumptions include attention to concept development, the need for a variety of materials to represent mathematical ideas and the need for a broad range of math content.

The writers of the Standards also remind us of the need for appropriate evaluation of children's progress in math learning.

Guides for Classroom Practice

The Standards imply and specify many guidelines for encouraging mathematics learning in young children. These guidelines pertain to children below the kindergarten level as well as those in Grades K - 4.

Involve children actively in real experiences

Children need to use concrete materials as they encounter mathematical ideas. Children must construct ideas for themselves; ideas that are generated and internalized by children are much better understood and remembered than ideas that adults have told to children and encouraged them to memorize.

For example, children need to use and arrange counters, classify objects into sets, line up objects and compare them, handle scales and learn to make things balance, cut playdough into pieces, and fill and empty containers. Watching adults do these things is not nearly as effective.

Present problem solving in a real-life context

Educators must help children deal with real problems as they arise in the classroom. Are there enough crackers for each child to have two? Children can solve this problem by placing napkins at each child's place, then passing out crackers to see if there are enough to "go around" twice.

"Is anyone absent today?" Children can help the teacher count and check. "How can we divide a square into two equal pieces?" Children can fold and cut paper squares and find many answers to the question.

Encourage children to use many language forms

Children can use oral language to describe what they are doing or to express questions. With questions such as " How did you do that?" and

"How do you know?", caregivers can encourage children to tell about their thinking and verify their work. Asking "How did you try...?" and "What else can you do?" encourages children to use language as they explore mathematics. Nonverbal language also communicates; teachers can ask children to "Show me how you did that." to help children express ideas without using words.

Other expressive forms that children can use in mathematics are pictures, collages, maps, graphs, and written words. Children should be exposed to a variety of language forms to develop the idea "We can show our ideas to others many different ways."

Help children to verify ideas for themselves rather than depending on adults

Being independent in mathematical thinking enhances children's reasoning abilities and self-confidence. It builds the idea "I can think and reason. Lots of times, I know and can show that I'm right."

As Lucy arranged plastic eggs in a basket with the numeral six on it, her teacher asked, "Lucy, how can you tell you have the right number there?" Lucy replied, "Well, I'll count them for you. I'll arrange them on this card with that many dots too."

Lucy was indeed sure of her math abilities. In some cases, children will recognize their own errors as they are asked to verify answers. Freddy was working with pipecleaner snakes, arranging them in order from longest to shortest.

His teacher asked, "Tell me about what you're doing." Freddy said, "Here's the long snake and then this one and then..." As Freddy came to a snake that was out of order, he rearranged it and went on with his narration.

A teacher's questions or requests to verify answers should not be directed only to children who are making mistakes; children could be asked to verify correct answers as well.

Evaluate children's progress in many ways

As adults attempt to assess children's prog-ress in mathematics, they should attempt to see how children are thinking as well as what the children can do. For young children, the thinking process is best assessed by talking to children and listening to them talking to each other (and themselves) as they work.

As adults make observations of children's work and work habits, they may want to make brief written notes to be filed, or they may want to mark a checklist on which skills and attitudes are listed.

Adults may set up situations where they work with children in small groups and ask the children to perform tasks such as identifying shapes, counting, classifying objects, and solving problems. Educators will also want to note attitudes such as curiosity, attention, eagerness to participate, and persistence as they try to evaluate children's growth in mathematics.

Mathematics Activities for Young Children

The following pages include descriptions of a variety of math activities for young children. Throughout the descriptions there are opportunities for young children to use reasoning and problem solving.

CLASSIFYING is making groups or sets on the basis of one or more characteristics. Children should work with materials and classify the same set of materials many different ways.

For example, as the children are studying "ourselves," they might see whether or not their shirts have fasteners. The children themselves could form two groups -- those with fasteners on their shirts and those without.

Next, the children could regroup themselves as those with plain shirts and those with patterned shirts. The children could then divide into those with long-sleeved shirts and those with short-sleeved shirts. Such activities let children see that there are many bases on which classifications can be made; it encourages flexible thinking.

Children can classify many things. Shells, buttons, blocks, rocks, leaves, flannel board pieces, plastic animal models, and jar lids are examples of commonly available materials that children can sort into groups.

Children can arrange the sets that they make on the floor or on a table top. They can arrange circles of yarn and place objects inside the yarn. Children can sort materials into small boxes or arrange the materials on a folder divided into sections. And adults can help children talk about the sets they are making and perhaps write labels for the sets.

Playing "What's My Rule" is fun and thought-provoking. A person sorts objects into categories by some characteristic that is not named. Others then try to sort other objects according to the same rule and guess what the rule is.

For example, the teacher might place several pennies into a pile and place other coins in another pile. Sandy might be given a penny to place in a pile. If Sandy chooses the penny pile, the teacher can say, "Sandy used the rule I was thinking of." If she did not, the teacher can say, "That's not the pile I was thinking of. Try again."

After several children have had a turn, the teacher can ask the children to tell what they thought the rule for classifying was -- copper coins and silvery coins or pennies and coins that are not pennies. Children can also be leaders in the "What's My Rule" game.

COMPARING is a skill that children use every day. When complaints are heard, "Her piece is bigger than mine!", early childhood educators are well aware of children's ability to compare. When children make comparisons, they deal with equality of sets or quantities; they may need to use greater than and less than relationships when comparing sets, too.

Besides comparing numbers of items, children can compare areas and volumes -- which covers the most surface or which takes up the most space? Children can also use concepts and words like taller and shorter, heavier and lighter, and wider and narrower as they make comparisons.

Educators can take advantage of many natural situations and ask children to make comparisons. As children arrive in the morning, adults can help children discuss who got to school earlier and later. Children can compare the lengths of their names as they write them. Joel might see that Guillermo's name has more letters than his does even before he can read both names.

As the weather changes, children can use words like warmer and cooler to describe the outdoor conditions. Children might compare a long walk they took to the shorter walk they take to their lunchroom.

Adults can also set up situations for children to make comparisons. Using a feely bag is fun and adds a touch of suspense to making comparisons. A caregiver might place pipecleaners of varying lengths in a feely bag and ask a child to feel inside and find a pipecleaner about as long as her hand. She can bring out the pipecleaner she has chosen

and make a direct comparison.

An adult might place a margarine container inside an old sock to make a feely box. The box could be filled with marbles. Each of two children could reach in and take a handful of marbles. Then, each can place his marbles in two rows on the rug or on a terry cloth towel. They can line up the marbles and see if the two sets of marbles have the same number or if one set has more than the other.

This use of one-to-one correspondence helps children make comparisons. It lets them verify whether sets are equal or not.

Use the children themselves as another interesting "thing" to compare. Pose questions such as these:

Are there more boys than girls in the classroom now or are there the same number? Let's line up and see.

Are more of us wearing long pants than short pants or skirts? Let's make some sets and find out.

Who wants a cookie and who wants a cracker? How do our sets of people compare? Each of these questions is also suitable for making a graph.

As children work with geometric shapes adults can help them compare the shapes by asking, "How are these alike? How are they different?". If children are working with shapes of cardboard, plastic, or wood, they can hold the shapes side by side to compare them.

To deal with concepts of lighter and heavier, children can gather many objects of varying weights. Adults can help the children hold the objects and try to tell if they weigh about the same or if one object seems heavier than another.

Adults should guide beginners to choose pairs of objects where the differences are fairly signifi-cant. Children can predict what will happen if the objects are placed on a simple balance scale and test their predictions. Adults can help them use language to describe the situation.

As educators present classifying situations to children, they should help them make compari-sons about their results. For example, children might arrange plastic animals into groups based on how they move -- those that walk, swim, fly, and crawl or slither. Once the animals are arranged, the children can tell which set has more animals or if any sets have the same number of animals.

As children discuss community helpers, the adult might have the children draw pictures. When the pictures are completed, the children can sort them into workers who wear uniforms and work-ers who do not. They then can compare the resulting sets.

ORDERING is arrang-ing objects along a continuum on the basis of one or more characteristics. The teacher might ask two children to stand and have the other children decide who is taller. The teacher then might call a third child and let the children decide how to arrange the third child so that the group of three is in order from tallest to shortest. Then, the teacher might call a few other children to join the group and continue the tallest to shortest arrangement.

The teacher might choose children with blue jeans and ask the children to decide how to arrange them from the lightest blue jeans to the darkest. Children might also be arranged by the length of their hair or the number of pigtails they have. Any "ties" might stand behind each other in line.

A caregiver might let the children choose a

starting point and throw cotton balls. The children can discuss whether one ball is closer, farther, or about the same distance from the starting point.

The children might cut yarn to represent the distance of their cotton balls from the starting point, then stretch out their strings and compare their lengths. The strings can be arranged in order from shortest to longest.

Children can work with ordering several kinds of manipulatives. For example, they can arrange paper dinosaurs in order from tallest to shortest or from shortest to longest. They can arrange pipecleaner snakes on branches. The longest snake can go on the longest branch, the second longest on the second longest branch and so on.

Children can add felt hats to clown faces and order the hats from widest to narrowest. They can place plastic flowers on vases from arranging the flowers in order from tallest to shortest. Children can also fill baby food jars to various levels with colored water and place the jars in order from the most to the least full.

At snack time, one might let children take spoonfuls of dry cereal pieces and place them on a napkin; the children can then discuss who has the most and least and if any have the same amount.

As the children line up to go places, they can play line games using ordinal numbers. For example, educators could give instructions such as the following.

The first child please wave to the others. The third person and the fifth person in line, please sit down. The person who's second to last, trade places with the last person.

While children are in line, you might also ask, "Do we have enough children for each to have a partner?" Get a prediction, then have each child take a partner -- a child next to her. If each child has a partner say, "That means we had an even number. Everyone has a partner. We can make pairs." If one child is left, let that child join another pair.

PATTERNING is another important mathematics skill. Patterning involves establishing a sequence and repeating that sequence. Patterning draws children's attention to regularities and lays a foundation for later understanding of more complex and abstract patterns in mathematics. Recognizing and using patterns is a valuable problem-solving tool.

As children work with patterns, a typical sequence of development is reproduction, identification or description, extension, and translation. First, a child should copy or reproduce a pattern made by someone else. This step involves examination of an existing pattern and checking of the pattern that is made. Then, a child can describe what he has done.

Rico's teacher had prepared task cards to go with small colored blocks. Rico selected a card and arranged some blocks below the blocks pictured on the card. He mumbled to himself, "red, red, green, red again, red, then green." When Rico's teacher asked, "Can you make the same pattern longer?" Rico was happy to oblige. He made a longer "train" of blocks.

The teacher asked some other children to look at Rico's pattern and tell about it. She said, "This pattern makes me think of...", Then she clapped, clapped, and snapped; she clapped, clapped, and snapped again as the children joined in. Thus they had translated the pattern a,a,b,a,a,b,a,a,b to another form -- from blocks to using body instruments.

Patterns may be presented visually, auditorially, or by using motor skills. Children can string beads or use blocks linked together to make patterns. They can work with a button collection and make patterns such as a large button, a small button, a large button, a small button. They can make patterns using the buttonholes as a stimulus-- for example two holes, two holes, two holes, four holes; two holes, two holes, two holes, four holes.

They might translate the last pattern by arranging children -- three seated, then one standing; three seated, then one standing.

Children can fill pegboards with pegs in patterns; they can copy patterns onto geoboards. They can make paper chains or link pipecleaners together using a repeatable pattern of colors.

Teachers can glue materials with tactile appeal to cards and let the children feel the cards, describe what they feel and tell or choose what would come next. For example, a teacher could make a pattern by gluing styrofoam bits and strips of sandpaper to a long piece of posterboard. A blindfolded child can feel the pattern and tell what

he feels, then choose, by feeling, another strip to continue the pattern of the first one.

Other materials to use for feely patterns are pieces of corduroy, metal bottle caps, and toothpicks.

The children themselves can also form patterns. They might form a pattern of one child seated, one child standing; one child seated, one child standing. The teacher can invite more children to join the group continuing the pattern. The children can keep time to music in a pattern; they can clap, clap, clap, pat; clap, clap, clap, pat to a record in 4/4 time, for example.

The teacher can invite various children to suggest other patterns for the group, then help the group follow the patterns that are suggested. As children are dismissed from group time to go to learning centers, the teacher might ask the first child to hop to the center of his choice, then ask the second child to carefully walk backwards, the third child to hop, the fourth child to walk backwards and so on. After several children have left, the teacher can ask the group what the next child should do.

As children become aware of patterns, they can look for patterns in the world around them. Floor and ceiling tiles are often laid in patterns that can be examined and described. The windows in a room may form a regular, repeated pattern. The children's clothing may include patterns. Kesha's striped shirt may have a wide stripe, then a narrow one for example. Willa's blouse may have a pattern of dots.

The children might see that the calendar has a repeatable sequence of days in each week. They might talk about the classroom schedule as a pattern that repeats itself most days. Morning, afternoon, and night also follow each other in a repeatable sequence or pattern.

NUMBERS AND NUMERALS are other important areas in mathematics in which young children need to work. Children must gain ideas of what numbers mean and learn to associate the number symbols (numerals) with quantities. Many six-year olds can learn number words as well.

Work with counting complements work with numbers and numerals and lays the basis for much mathematical thinking. For most children, progress in counting proceeds in this sequence: rote counting, rational counting, and skip counting. Rote counting is the ability to say number names in a correct sequence. It does not necessarily indicate that children have any idea of number meanings.

Rational counting is the ability to count members in a set saying one number name for each member. It will help many children to count rationally if they move objects as they say a single number name.

For example, they can push blocks from one pile to another as they count; they can move flannel board pieces from one pile to another. When a group of people is counted, they can move from one place to another, or sit as each one is counted.

For six-year olds, some skip counting can be introduced. Counting by twos or fives are examples of skip counting. To help children learn to skip count by twos, educators might have them line up in pairs, then have the group count the first partner in each pair saying the number name very quietly and the second number name loudly -- one, TWO, three. FOUR, five, SIX, and so on. As each pair is counted, they should move a short distance away from the group that is yet to be counted. After some practice, the children can say the odd numbers silently and the even numbers out loud. Finally, they can say just the even numbers.

Children can practice skip counting by fives in a similar way. They might count all the

fingers of the children at each table; they might each hold five crayons and skip count the crayons.

Work with numbers can be constant in the early childhood classroom. Children can count the number of people in the room and choose a card to display showing the number of children and adults in attendance. They can count the number of children who are wearing certain kinds of clothes and help to record their findings. Caregivers might use a version of "London Bridge" for a short counting game.

If you're wearing plaid, stand up.
Plaid, stand up; plaid stand up.

If you're wearing plaid, stand up.
How many are there?

(Continue for other patterns such as stripes, "plains," animal patterns, and so on.)

To work with numbers and numerals, children can use many different kinds of games. Educators can make little place mats and then children can spoon out dry macaroni and brown ball fringe pieces to represent spaghetti and meatballs. The children can count what they have on their plates and choose numerals cards to show the numbers. They can also work from task cards that tell how much of each "food" to take with pictures or numerals.

Another food-oriented game is number sand-

wiches. Teachers can prepare felt or paper sandwich "ingredients" -- bread, buns, lunch meat, hamburgers, cheese, lettuce, catsup, and so on. The pieces can have numerals and number symbols on them. The children stack up pieces to make sandwiches of pieces that represent the same number. Also, the teacher can ask the children to count the number of ingredients in their sandwiches and ask questions such as "You have seven pieces. If you added two more how many would you have?"

Paper plates can form the basis for many number games. Paper plates can be numbered, and the children can arrange the appropriate number of playdough or paper foods on the plates. Children can place "personal-sized" paper pizzas with numbers of pieces of pepperoni or pepper on the appropriate plates. Numbered plates can become "pens" or "cages" in which to place plastic animals. Plates can serve as containers for arranging appropriate numbers of flowers, leaves, or rocks. Other number-numeral games can be developed around unit themes or seasonal motifs. For a unit on sports, children can match numbered football helmets and footballs or catchers mitts and baseballs.

For a unit on dinosaurs, children can match cutouts of dinosaur mothers with the appropriate number of dinosaurs eggs or babies. They can arrange dinosaurs with spots in caves marked with numerals.

They can arrange plastic eggs in numbered baskets or match bunnies marked with numerals to Easter eggs marked with numbers of dots. Most materials designed for work with numbers and numerals can also be put in numerical order. Numbers of objects can also be compared.

Children should create their own number books. They can make a page for each of several numbers, or they could make a book of a single number like five. In the books, children can show numbers many different ways.

They can draw pictures. They can cut and paste pictures of objects on the pages. They can print on the pages with stamp pad printers or print appropriate numbers of finger prints on the pages. They can glue materials such as toothpicks, scraps of fabric, or styrofoam bits to the pages. Children's number books can be placed in the class library center to be read before children take them home.

As the teacher works with numbers and numerals, be sure to include many songs and fingerplays that involve numbers. One can add to children's knowledge of numbers by using books, too. Many excellent picture and story books are available.

For instance, Hague's **Numbears** (1986) presents representations of the numbers 1 through 12 in a story with fanciful teddy bears as characters. **Who's Counting** (Tarfuri, 1986) features a dog and her puppies that appear on pages along with various numbers of other creatures.

After reading a book like one of these, the children might work in groups and make their own number books based on an animal theme. They might also assemble sets of stuffed animals or animal models to represent numbers.

To accompany a book, the teacher might make a number pocket chart of clear plastic material. Children can put number cards in the pockets and place the appropriate numbers of objects in the pockets.

Problem solving is a vital area of mathematics. People encounter and solve problems continually. Problems are situations in which answers are not readily apparent; rather problems take some thought and testing of solutions. Problem solving requires application of skills to new and challenging situations. For young children these situations should be concrete. Often, they should be solvable by manipulation and trial and error.

Early childhood educators can help children develop their abilities in concrete problem solving by presenting a variety of problems and expecting the children to solve them. Educators can establish the confidence that is necessary for problem solving, also. Problem solving can occur in every area of the curriculum as well as in social situations.

Suppose the class is making Valentine baskets out of gallon milk jugs. Several children have volunteered to bring jugs and the teacher's assistant has also brought some jugs. There is quite a large pile of jugs, so the teacher asks the children, "Do we have enough jugs for everyone to have one? Each of you needs a jug and so do Mrs. Brown and I."

If the children do not suggest answers to the

problem, help them clarify the situation; "What are we trying to find out? Who can tell what the problem is?" If the children are still "blank," help them in a concrete way: "Amy needs a jug. Paul needs a jug. LaShurn needs a jug...How many will we need in all?"

The children might suggest passing out the jugs to see if there are enough. Someone might also suggest counting people, counting jugs, and comparing numbers. Let the children carry out at least one solution to the problem.

If there are not enough jugs, pose another problem, "How can we get more jugs so we will have enough?"

Children can solve many problems as they work with classroom materials. "Do we have enough?" problems of the type previously discussed occur often. More examples are:

"Do we have enough markers for each person to have two?"

"Here are our pattern blocks. Do we have enough for each of us to get 6 blocks?"

If there are left-overs, the teacher can ask "What can we do with them?"

"Do we have enough cars to put two in each garage?"

Work with plastic animals sets the stage for much problem solving. You might ask the children to classify the animals many different ways. They might group the animals by color, by whether they can fly or not, by whether they are wild or tame, by whether they have long necks or not, and so on.

The caregiver could suggest little animal stories.

"Suppose the zookeeper had 12 animals and 2 were loaned to another zoo, how many animals would be left?"

"If the zookeeper started with 8 animals and got 3 more, how many would there be?"

"If we had just 5 cages, how could we arrange our 12 animals?"

An adult might help children work a variety of problems with blocks. One could draw block outlines on a piece of paper to specify the start of a building or tower. The children could see what different designs they can make based on the designated starting arrangement.

The adult might sketch a simple design and ask children to actually build what the design shows. Children could use small colored blocks and see how many ways they can arrange five blocks in a row. They might color on a recording sheet to show their designs.

Educators could set up a store in the dramatic play area. The children could mark prices on items 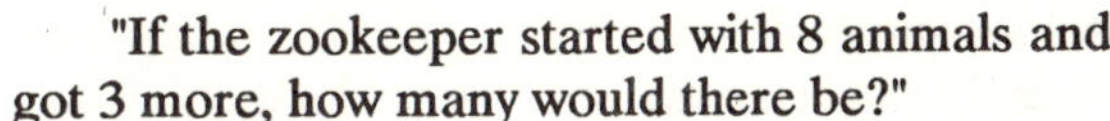 using pictures of coins, coin rubbings, or by taping on play money. Customers can have play money to spend. They can decide what they want to buy and decide if they have enough of the right kinds of coins to do so. This process will involve a good deal of counting, comparing, and decision-making.

GEOMETRY surrounds children. As they look about the world they see many flat and three-dimensional shapes. With the adult they can examine their component parts -- lines, angles and surfaces -- or they can look and compare shapes as wholes.

As they explore geometry, children should use many different kinds of models -- real world models, teacher-made and commercially-made models, and models the children themselves make. As they work with geometry, children use classifying and observing skills, and they learn new words.

Children might begin work in geometry by

making shapes of various materials. They can make balls (spheres), rolls (cylinders), and flat shapes of playdough or clay. They can cut around cardboard or plastic figures to make shape "cookies." As they work, they can compare sizes and other characteristics of their creations.

They can see and discuss which shapes have corners (angles) and which shapes have curved parts and flat or straight parts. As adults work with children, the adults should use as many geometric words as possible. They should encourage children to use geometric vocabulary as well as to describe the shapes in less formal language.

As children work with shapes, they should find as many real-world shapes as possible. Educators might picture each of several shapes on half-poster boards and let the children suggest real objects that have those shapes. Add names to the posters over a period of days as the children suggest things.

Many foods -- peas, cut green beans, oranges, hamburgers, crackers -- are in recognizable geometric shapes. An adult might suggest that the children think about foods if they do not mention them. Take the children on a shape walk around the school and play yard to look for and make note of more shapes.

Children can make their own pictures of geometric shapes of many different materials. They can arrange yarn on a flannel board in freeform shapes or duplicate shapes from task cards. Educators should ask children to describe their shapes as the children work.

Children can arrange strip magnets or bits of magnets on magnet boards, file cabinet surfaces, or old steel cookie sheets to form geometric shapes. They can trace geometric figures in a sand or salt tray. They can paint on easel paper cut in various shapes.

triangle

circle

square

Children can create geometric designs from many materials. Pattern blocks, felt pieces, and stamp pads are commonly available supplies that can be used. Children can make collage designs of precut paper shapes. They can make designs on geoboards following task card designs, duplicating designs created by classmates, or making up their own patterns.

Children can also form models of geometric shapes using their hands and bodies. The teacher can whisper the name of a shape to a group of children; those children can form the shape with their bodies for the others to name and describe.

Children will enjoy a "mystery shape rub." Caregivers can cut many geometric shapes of poster board or sandpaper. The shapes can be placed on a table top and covered with butcher paper that is taped in place. The children can come to the table, feel for a place to start, then use the sides of crayons to rub over and disclose the figures that are hidden below. The group might write a story about what shapes they found. They could make a graph showing how many of each shape were "uncovered." Children who are interested can also make their own shape books tracing and rubbing shapes on the pages.

MEASUREMENT is a process that lets people compare sizes, temperatures, volumes, and weights. Measurement links a number and a unit. For instance, a child may be 80 centimeters tall. A container may hold 12 fluid ounces. A stack of books may weigh 1800 grams.

For young children, most work with measurement should involve making comparisons of quantities, ordering them, and using nonstandard measurements.

Adults can help children use standard measurements as parts of cooking activities and gathering data. For the early 1990s, children in our country will study both the metric system and "inch-pound" or customary measurement system when they are in elementary school. Often the metric system is presented first in textbooks because it relates well to our decimal number system. Early childhood educators will probably want to use both systems as they work with young children.

Starting children with comparisons of quantities is easy. Children can choose an object, find an object that is larger (or taller or wider), then find a third object that is larger still, and a fourth still larger object to add to the collection.

Children can put a little sand in a bag and feel the bag to note its weight. They can put more sand in a second bag and feel that it is heavier than the first. A group of children can make a series or four or five bags for their classmates, close the bags, and let classmates feel the bags and try to put them in order from heaviest to lightest.

Children might put their hands in several containers of water of varying temperatures and try to tell which water is the warmest and the coolest. Changes in the temperature outdoors can be noted and discussed. Adults can help small groups of five- and six-year olds take the temperature with a thermometer.

Children should predict and verify their judgements as they work with measurement concepts. A teacher can ask one child from a group to stand, then let the children identify another seated child whom they think will be taller than the child who is standing. The children could show with their hands about how much taller they think the child they have chosen will be. The second child can then stand next to the first one, and the children can compare their predictions to the actual heights of their two classmates.

Then, the teacher could call for a prediction of a a child who is about "this much" (show them) shorter than the second child. The group could select someone; the child can stand and let the children compare their guesses to the actual sizes.

For a variation on the predict and verify game, the teacher might show a strip of paper and ask several children to leave the group and bring back objects about as long as the paper. As the children bring the objects, they can be directly compared to the paper strip. The children can tell whether each object is about as long as the strip, or longer or shorter.

The teacher might show a bag or suitcase and ask the children to name and show objects that would fit inside and objects that are too large to fit. The children should verify some of the suggestions.

At the sand table, the teacher might show a container and ask the children to scoop up about enough sand to fit in the container. The children can take turns pouring sand into the container and seeing if their estimates were close or not.

In measurement activities like these, language that compares things should abound. Words like "very close," "about right," "too much," "bigger," "hotter," and "lighter" are all words that children can learn to use if they have opportunities to do so.

Children can gather measurement data at home. For example, the instructor at school might help children trace around their feet and cut out their footprints. The children can take the prints home with the request to trace family members' feet and bring the tracings to school.

At school the children can discuss the tracings; teachers can help them label each print with the name of a family member and cut them out. The children can work in groups to compare their prints and place them in order from shortest to longest. The teacher might ask, "Whose print is this -- could it be Yi's mother or could it be her baby sister?" The prints can be displayed on a bulletin board or taped to the floor for the children to compare to their own feet.

Helping children measure the lengths of things using nonstandard measurements is good. Any easily-available object makes a nonstandard measuring device. For example, the length of a table can be measured in hands (held lengthwise or crosswise), blocks, or crayon lengths.

In a classroom with concrete block walls, each child's height might be measured in blocks. All measurement has errors. It is fine to refer to a child's height as "between 6 and 7 blocks" or "just less then 7 blocks."

Children can make paper clip chains and use them to measure things such as the classroom rug, the height of a chair, or the distance around a tin can. Children can use paper strips to measure lengths of small objects. Caregivers can help children to record data about measurements as they work.

COLLECTING DATA AND MAKING AND INTERPRETING GRAPHS is complementary to work with classifying, comparing, developing number meanings, and using numerals. Educators can present graphing experiences often; for each unit that is taught, several graphs can be used to extend and summarize the children's work.

Young children can work with real graphs -- graphs in which real things or people are arranged in categories. They can also work with picture graphs and several versions of bar graphs. Usually, graphs with two categories are easiest for beginners. After some experiences, children can work successfully with graphs that use three or more categories.

For real graphs, educators might prepare a large plastic graph grid using strips of shelf paper, a tablecloth, or a sheet of plastic. The grid can be used for a variety of real graphs. For example, the children might stand on the categories of the graph holding name cards to show whether their first names have five or fewer letters or more than five letters.

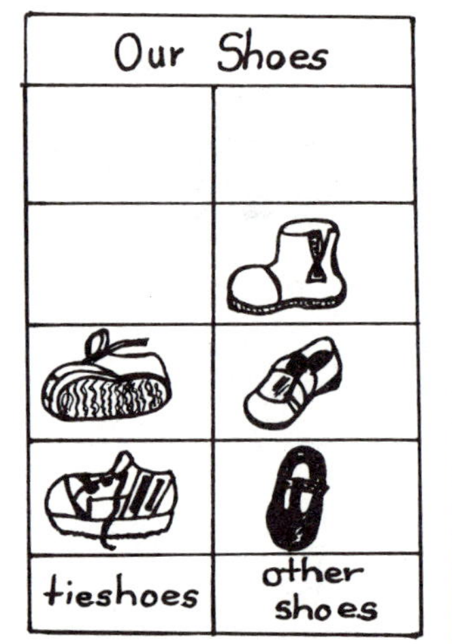

Children could also arrange themselves on the graph grid to show whether they rode to school in a car or not. Children could arrange themselves on the graph grid to show which they would choose -- a taco or a grilled chicken sandwich.

The real graph grid can also be used for placing objects. Each child might select an object from a mystery bag and arrange it on the grid to show if the shape is a triangle or a circle. Each child could choose a crayon from a box and arrange the crayons in "red" and "blue" categories. Children can each remove a shoe and place the shoes in "tie shoes" and "other shoes" categories.

Graphs should be labeled with titles and category names. Often the children can help to decide what the titles should be. Titles and category names can be written on paper and placed or clipped to graph forms.

As the children make graphs, the teacher should help them interpret the graphs. Asking a general question such as "What does our graph tell us?" often results in many different answers. Teachers can then ask specific questions to pursue data not noted by the children. Questions such as "How many are in this category?", "Do any categories have the same number?", and "How many things are on our graph in all?" are often appropriate.

Bar graphs can be designed in horizontal or vertical formats. Children can make vertical bar graphs on paper, or they may pile up blocks or milk cartons to represent themselves. Teachers may want to help children make reusable graph markers to use again and again on bar graphs. These markers could be photos or pictures of the children, juice cans decorated and personalized to represent children, clothespins with children's names, or name cards.

Educators may want to prepare blank reusable bar graph grids like the real graph grids previously described. Titles and category names can be temporarily attached to the forms.

For bar graphs, children might draw on paper plates their choice

of something to eat at snack time -- cookies, raisins, or crackers might be choices. They then can arrange the paper plates on a graph grid to show their preferences.

Children could attach clothespins to a graph grid to show whether they think it will rain over the weekend or not. They can pile up blocks with their names to show whether they prefer to play in the blocks or dramatic play area.

Children can draw pictures and arrange the pictures to make a pictograph. Each child might draw a picture of something with square corners that is found in the classroom. The children can display their pictures and arrange them in categories to show squares, rectangles, and other shapes with right angles.

Children's pictures of themselves can be ar-

ranged on pictographs to show such differences as whether a child would rather play outdoors or watch television after school or whether a child went shopping over the weekend or not.

After a trip to the zoo, or after watching a special animal movie, children can draw pictures of their favorite animals and display the pictures as a pictograph.

After the class has had many experiences with graphing, caregivers can organize teams of two and three children to poll their classmates and make a graph of their opinions. A pair of children can work with the teacher to decide on a suitable topic for a graph.

They might plan to ask their classmates to choose whether they prefer chocolate or white milk. The caregiver can help the children mark symbols for the two kinds of milk on a small graph form. The "pollsters" can then go around the room and ask their classmates for their choices and help each child mark a block on the graph. The caregiver can help the "pollsters" show their results at a large group time.

In few days another pair of children might take a poll on whether or not their classmates are wearing belts.

LEARNING ABOUT TIME AND MONEY is another area in which young children can grow. References to time and money are common in our society. Although time and money concepts are complex and develop slowly over a period of time, early childhood educators can help children build a strong foundation in these areas.

Children see adults spending money and hear them discussing it. To help them gain ideas of the value and uses of money, You might talk about things that can be purchased and things that are not bought and sold. Smiles, hugs, and kind words are valuable things that people share and give away rather than buy. Sunshine and rain cannot be purchased either.

"What do people buy and spend money for?" Help children compile a long list. Most children will be familiar with spending money on food, toys, entertainment, and gasoline. Some may mention rent, utility bills, and services as things that their families spend money on.

Educators can help children become familiar with coins and their names. They might place several different coins in ziplock bags and draw a circle with permanent marker on the bags. Children can examine and compare the coins and notice their differences in color and the fact that coins have two different sides.

The teacher may ask children to slide a coin like one that shown into the circle and name the coin and tell its value in pennies. The children might be told to slide a dime into the circle and tell how they identified the dime. Different children may move a coin into the circle and the others can select the same coin and name it.

When the children feel coins, they may notice that dimes and quarters have little grooves on their edges called reeding. They may pick up the coin that is largest, smallest, thickest, and thinnest in a set. Several kinds of coins may be placed in a feely bag and children asked to take turns choosing coins that an adult describes. Once a child selects a coin, the others may name the coin.

Set up a drive-in store in your dramatic play area. Children could "drive through" in cars made of boxes with the bottoms cut out. Prices for items to be sold can be marked on them with coin pictures. Customers must pay for their purchases by matching coins and counting out the correct numbers.

For six-year olds, a chart might be made that shows coin exchanges. If customers do not have "correct change," they can trade coins (2 nickels for a dime, for example) getting information from the chart. Children should be encouraged to discuss the coins and their names as they work.

Children might make little banks from milk cartons and mark them with coin pictures, coin names, and numerals. Then, the children may place the appropriate coins or coin rubbing pictures in the banks. Educators can help children make banks to take home and use to keep their money.

Caregivers might plan a field trip to a grocery store or another store and arrange to buy something. The children can shop for the item and notice its price. Adults can point out price tags on other items and ask children to read some of the prices. Educators should help the children pay for the item, look at the change, and at the receipt.

To develop time concepts, teachers can help children discuss events that happen in the school day."What happens first? What event comes next? Last in the day?"

Teachers might help children draw a long time line and divide it into hourly segments. They may help children decide what events typically occur in the time segments and draw pictures to represent events in the daily routine. They might discuss events that take a long time and those that can be completed in shorter periods of time.

The instructor could draw children's attention to the clock and the positions of its hands during the day. If a digital clock is available, the children can practice reading it. Educators can tell them about the time; for example, 1:45 says that soon it will be two o'clock.

Children can make paper clocks with cardboard hands fastened on with a brad. Caregivers can help children set their clocks to various times, emphasizing times on the hour and half hour. The children can discuss things they might be doing at the times shown on the clocks; at 7:00 a child may get up. At 2:00, he may be outdoors playing.

To help children learn about time units such as months and seasons, educators might make small posters and each month children can gather materials outdoors and glue them to the posters. They can help to write some short notes about events that occurred in each month.

As the year progresses, they may look at them and make notes about changes in seasons as special events occur. Six year olds might make individual and group books about the changes in months and seasons.

Math an Area of Importance, an Area for Growth

Mathematics is an area in which all children can grow and progress. Teachers can enhance their growth by presenting math concepts in a variety of interesting and concrete ways. Educators must integrate math activities into each unit of study. They must be sure to encourage children to talk about what they are doing. Whenever possible, educators should ask children to verify their own answers and show how they arrived at answers.

Symbols should be presented in meaningful contexts rather than in isolation. Math is challenging and fun. Early childhood educators have wonderful opportunities to help children develop concepts, skills and positive attitudes in this area.

Chapter 5

Science for Young Children

The study of science is perfectly suited to the needs and interests of young children. Children are curious and learn by investigating and exploring. They pose questions for themselves and for adults. Often they try to answer their own questions by manipulating objects and experimenting.

Science experiences for young children can be as diverse as playing and "messing about" in mud, listening to a flannel board story about winter, or using a magnet to see which objects are attracted to it. As children explore and take part in science activities planned by adults, they are exposed to and use a vocabulary rich in descriptive, science-oriented words. They have occasions to practice some of the same behaviors that scientists use as they work.

What We Know

Children learn more about science when they are actively involved than they do when science is presented as a series of facts. Involvement also enhances children's attitudes toward science and toward learning in general. The National Science Teachers Association document Criteria for Excellence (1987) stresses the need for hands-on experiences for young children. Instruction should offer many problem-solving experiences and present activities that are relevant to the lives of children.

Exemplary science programs (Penick and Yager, 1983) are those that are designed to be excellent rather than merely acceptable. They depend on curriculum developed by teachers; often staff members are involved in inservice training and programs that focus on science. Exemplary programs stress science content, science process, and development of positive, responsible attitudes. Time, efforts, and resources are devoted to science teaching.

The National Science Teachers Association (Anderson, 1989) is concerned about opportunities in science education for all children -- boys, girls, children of all social classes, races, and ethnic groups. Early childhood educators share these same concerns. By presenting science as inviting, interesting, and relevant, people who work with young children can lay a firm foundation of knowledge, skills, and attitudes for children's later work. They help to prevent later problems for children. Attention to science deserves an important part in the early childhood curriculum.

Guides for Classroom Practice

Based on NSTA guidelines, several suggestions can guide educators as they plan and implement science activities for four- through six-year old children.

Think active involvement

Experts agree that involvement of children is essential. "Concrete," "hands-on," and "active learning" are terms that should be synonymous with science for young children. Children are not passive receivers of knowledge. Instead, they must construct knowledge for themselves. Otherwise science becomes something to be memorized to please an adult and is soon forgotten.

Balance science content

Many teachers feel comfortable with life sciences--the study of plants, animals, the human body, health, and nature. They must also be attuned to the many opportunities they can provide for children to work with environmental science as they study the earth about them, the weather, and space. The physical sciences also offer interesting topics such as water, air, magnets, machines, and light for involvement and exploration.

*Provide opportunities for children
to use science processes*

Science processes such as observing, communicating, predicting, and classifying can be used in many ways to help children learn science and to practice the ways that scientists work. Ways that children can use several science processes are presented later in this chapter. Teachers and curriculum planners must consider science process as well as science content as they plan for children.

Cultivate children's attitudes about science

Besides science content and process, an essential third area of consideration is attitude. Dispositions such as interest, curiosity, responsibility, and willingness to base conclusions on evidence can be enhanced with good science programs and activities for young children. Positive attitudes are inseparable from science content and use of process. The three areas are complementary.

When science content--facts and concepts-- are presented in ways that involve children and let them use science processes, children learn and retain information as they learn to learn. They adopt attitudes that they can and want to learn more. Thus, science for young children should be a blend of content, process, and attitude development.

*Provide real objects for young children
to handle and explore*

Science helps people describe and understand the world around tham. Young children are concrete learners; thus, a variety of materials and specimens are necessary to enhance their learning.

Use immediate surroundings as a basis for science

Children can learn much from the plants around them, animals in the school yard (worms, spiders, insects), and the neighborhood with its soil, rocks, buildings, machines. and tools. Objects need not be expensive or exotic. Leaves from the school ground, water and clean plastic containers, and sunlight and rain can be used in many ways to help young children gain understanding of their world.

*Supplement experiences with objects
by using books, pictures, television, other media*

Children are interested in African animals, space travel, and weather at the North Pole. Though most children cannot directly experience these things, caregivers can build their knowledge by choosing a variety of media.

*Take advantage of unplanned, spontaneous
opportunities for teaching and learning*

While many planned activities in science are desirable, educators must be open to the potential of unplanned occurrences such as the appearance of a large toad in the school yard, a newscast of a space flight on television, or a hail storm.

*Help children develop and practice
life-long habits*

In science, educators stress the need for good habits such as exercise, healthy diet, and brushing teeth. Children then must practice these habits at school and at home. Adults can set the stage by serving healthy snacks, encouraging all children to take part in active games, and providing a time and place for children to brush their teeth after eating.

Explore big ideas in concrete ways

Concepts such as the process of growth and change, the characteristics of living things, and the regular and predictable interactions of objects have countless ramifications and examples in science. Caregivers can help children explore these ideas in concrete ways in science.

Science Activities
for Young Children

On the following pages readers will find descriptions of many science activities for young children. The first activities are organized around the science processes they promote. The science processes discussed are versions of those presented by the American Association for the Advancement of Science for Young Children. The second series of activities present a variety of things educators can do to expose children to various ideas and topics in science.

Science Activities Emphasizing Process

OBSERVING is using the senses to gain information about objects and events. As children examine objects, they should be encouraged to look at them closely, but also to feel the objects and see if the objects make sounds. They can smell the objects and, if appropriate, taste clean, safe objects to find out more about them.

As children observe, they should be encouraged to use both quantitative and qualitative observations. Quantitative observations concern numbers or amounts. If children have gathered rocks and want to know how many there are, it is clearer and more precise to say that there are seven rocks than to say many rocks.

Qualitative observations concern the qualities of objects. What colors are they? What textures can be seen and felt? What sizes and shapes are they? As children examine and describe objects, adults can help them make full, detailed observations by encouraging them to address a number of qualities of the objects.

If child says a rock is smooth, the adult might help the child be even more specific by asking, "As smooth as what? As smooth as glass? As smooth as your cheek?" Comparison help people to use language as they make qualitative statements.

Children might observe in an outdoor setting.

They could be seated and close their eyes and listen carefully for a full minute. Then the teacher could lead the children to quietly discuss all the things they heard.

Were some sounds made by people? Which sounds were made by natural phenomenon such as the wind or by animals? After the discussion, children might be encouraged to be quiet and listen again and see if they can hear any sounds they did not notice the first time. The children could then smell the air and describe and odors they detect. They could find and sniff a variety of natural objects--a freshly broken twig, some pine needles, or some new flowers.

The children could also lie on their backs and look at the treetops and the sky. After the experience of observing with many senses, the teacher could help the children write a group composition or draw pictures of some of the things they observed.

COMMUNICATING occurs in many forms as children work in science. They receive and convey ideas through oral and written language as well as body language. For example, as children stand outdoors in a strong spring breeze, they can describe how they know that the wind is blowing. They can show with hands and body movements what the breeze does to trees and the grass.

Caregivers can write down some of the children's descriptive words. Communications also may take the form of pictures, graphs, charts, diagrams, and maps. Communication plays a vital role in science as it does in the rest of children's lives.

After a walk on a balmy spring day, children can write or draw their reactions to being out of doors in the springtime. They might use the sand table and recreate a map or model of some of the places they visited on their walk. If spring leaves and flowers are in bloom, the children might pick some and use these to embellish their map. The children might discuss all the things they saw on their walk and show their favorite parts of the walk on a graph.

PREDICTING AND INFERRING are science processes that often can be used together. Predicting is telling in advance what one thinks will happen in a given situation. Inferring is making generalizations about phenomenon after an observation or experiment.

Often, predicting generates interest and curiosity in the outcomes of experiments. Taking a minute to predict encourages children to think and speculate. Caregivers should take the time to write down children's predictions about situations often so the group can refer back to these predictions.

Making inferences helps learners recall what happened and try to make some statements about the situation in general. Inferences often refer to science content that educators want children to remember.

To encourage children to predict and infer, a teacher might bring a small inflated balloon or two to the water table or water play area. She could ask the children to discuss what they think will happen if the balloons are placed in the water and how the balloons will react if they are placed under the water.

After listening to several children's ideas the teacher can let the children experiment with them. The teacher's role at this point is minimal. She insures that every child has a turn handling the balloons and listening. After several minutes of experimentation, the teacher might ask the children to describe what happened.

"Did the balloons always pop out of the water when they were submerged? Was there any way to make the balloons sink?"

The teacher might help the children make some conclusions about the way other balloons might behave in water. She might ask the children to extend their thinking to other air-filled objects.

"What would happen if we placed an inflated ball in the water? If we blew air into a plastic bag, tied the bag shut, then placed it in the water, what would happen?"

The children's discussion might lead to other things to try and discuss; that is the nature of science.

CLASSIFYING means making groups on the basis of one or more characteristics or qualities. Classifying is important in everyday life, in language, and in mathematics. Classifying demands that learners observe objects, notice their characteristics, then focus on one characteristic and decide how to separate the objects into groups.

On a spring day a caregiver might take the children to an area where they could gather some natural specimens. Each child could choose one specimen from the ground, one from an area above the child's waist, and one specimen found growing at about the children's waist level.

As they gather specimens the children are using a classification scheme. The children could bring their specimens to a central area and classify them further using the sense of touch. The children might divide the specimens into three groups-- those that are soft, those that are hard, and those that have both hard and soft textures.

The teacher might help the children decide on

some of their specimens that would be safe to take into the classroom and display.

USING TIME AND SPACE RELATION-SHIPS, numbers and math skills are inherent as children work with materials in science.

Children use time and space relationships when they deal with duration, size, shape, motion, symmetry, position, area, and volume. Work with time and space relationships and with numbers should be presented to children in varied and concrete ways

As they work with science activities, children can time events and deal with time concepts. For example, the children might closely watch a gold fish breathing and count the number of times its mouth or gills open and close in a minute. The children might watch the fish for a minute, discuss their results, and then gather data for another minute and compare it to their first minute's results.

Children might carefully fold leaves along the center vein and see if the two halves "match;" if they do, the leaf is symmetrical with respect to its center line.

Children might cover a large leaf with small blocks to approximately the area of the leaf.

In an outdoor setting, the children might choose some landmarks such as trees or bushes. They can stand in a location and predict how many giant steps they can take to reach the landmarks. Different children can take turns stepping off the distance and counting the number of steps it takes. They could record their results.

The teacher can help the children make comparative statements to describe the positions of the landmarks.

"We're closer to the tree than to the bush" or "The bush is shorter than the tree."

USING SEVERAL SCIENCE PROCESSES is possible in most science activities appropriate for children, educators should realize. For example, in a unit on healthy habits, one aspect might be focus on healthy foods. The children might sample raw vegetable snacks--slivers of zucchini, turnips, and carrots; radishes; celery sticks.

They can talk about the colors and shapes of the vegetables and describe how the vegetables crunch as they are eaten. The children can predict which vegetable will be the group's favorite.

After tasting, the children can place felt cutouts on a flannel board to show their favorites. The children can compile a list of vegetables they have tasted. They can classify the vegetables into two groups--green vegetables and those that are not green.

As they work with water, children can also use several science processes. They can feel the wetness and coolness of water and hear it gurgle and splash as it is poured. They can observe that water flows and takes the shape of any container into which it is poured.

They can see that water levels vary in different containers and also change as the containers are tilted and shaken (time and space relationships).

The children might make a "water clock" by cutting or punching a small hole near the bottom of a gallon milk container. They can predict how long it will take the water to flow out of the container.

Working outdoors or over a tub, the gallon can be filled with water. The children can count the time it takes for the water to drip out. They can also affix a piece of tape on the gallon; as the water flows out, the children can make a mark on the tape after each time they count to ten.

After seeing what happens to the water, the children might infer that it takes a longer time for water to flow from a container with a small hole; it would flow more rapidly from a container with a larger hole. A caregiver could help the children write a group composition about their experiences.

Science Activities Emphasizing Life Sciences

For young children, the study of living things includes attention to plants, animals, and the human body. Children can learn that all living things have common characteristics--growth, response to stimuli, use of food, and movement.

Children can be engaged in growing and caring for plants. They can see some of the wide variety of plants that grow in our world. They can begin to learn about the many ways that people use plants.

Children can also be introduced to a wide vari-

ety of animal life. They will learn that although different animals have different habits and needs, all share the same characteristics of living things that people have.

Study of the relationships of animals to people is also rich with possibilities to enhance young children's learning. Children also love to learn about themselves and other people. Science can include study of the human body--its parts and its functions--as well as ways to keep the body healthy and strong.

Following are descriptions of some of the many things children can do when life sciences are the focus of their science study.

WE'RE ALIVE! Over a period of several days, educators can introduce to children some charac-teristics of living things. A teacher could use a doll to compare to a child. Each child could ask a family member to show the child how large he was when he was born.

The children could show each other what they found out about their "baby sizes" and compare these sizes to those of the doll. The children could talk about how they have grown and how large they expect to be someday.

They could discuss the fact that their hair and fingernails grow and must be cut regularly. As living things, people respond to stimuli. An educator could plan with a child to do something funny for the group. The children could discuss their reactions to the funny actions of their classmate.

The teacher could "unexpectedly" drop a book with a loud bang, see how the children react, and then discuss their reactions with them. The children could discuss the fact that the doll does not grow or react.

Living things use food. The children could talk about foods they like and make a collage of pictures of healthy foods. They could fold paper plates in half, then in fourths. On each fourth the children could draw or glue a healthy food picture.

Different groups of children could help the teacher to prepare and serve healthy snacks to the other children. Parents could be invited to come to the classroom and help to prepare healthy foods from different heritages.

The doll does not need food; although it is fun to pretend to feed the doll, it cannot use food as a living thing does.

Living things move. They move in different

ways and at different speeds. Caregivers could use music of different tempos and invite the children to move and dance to the music.

The children could "dance" with different body parts; they could do an arm dance, a foot dance, a head dance, or an elbow dance. Children could move slowly, then very fast, then slowly again.

If the doll is invited to dance, it cannot do so on its own.

After several experiences with characteristics of living things, the care-giver might help the children conclude that the doll is not a living thing.

HEALTHY HABITS can be presented to children using pictures, felt board pieces, and demonstrations.

For example, a teacher might use a felt doll, show its pajamas, and illustrate how the doll can brush its teeth before going to bed. The children could then use the doll and its props and tell their own versions of a healthy bedtime routine.

But children also need opportunities to "role-play" healthy habits and actually practice the habits. Caregivers could help the children set up a dental clinic in the dramatic play area. They can provide mirrors for the children to examine their teeth.

Children should have opportunities to brush their teeth after meals at school. It might be part of the regular routine to wash hands before lunch, eat, then brush teeth before rest time.

Exercise is essential for healthy bodies. Many of today's children do not get enough exercise. Early childhood educators should provide many opportunities for children to exercise each day. Exercises can take the form of slow stretching to creative movement to marching to music to run-ning in the play yard.

Educators might set up an obstacle course and show the children how to perform such physical activities as run around milk cartons "pylons," jump across a barrier marked with rope, walk a balance beam, and hop from one location to an-other.

Regular exercise builds muscles and coordination, and it also lets children work off energy so that they are ready for quieter classroom activities.

HOW DO THEY WORK? WHAT DO THEY DO? Different body parts have different functions and work in different ways. Educators can help children learn these concepts by discussing them and letting the children demonstrate.

For example, eyes let people see. The children could discuss the many things they can see with their eyes. They can discuss the protection that eyelids and eyelashes provide, then work these body parts.

As a follow-up to discussion, children can make pictures of different body parts and their functions.

After discussing the fact that the mouth, throat, stomach, and intestines all have parts in helping the body eat and use food, the children could make a life-sized drawing of a body, draw the approximate locations of organs, and cut pictures of lots of good foods to glue on the stomach area of the figure.

SENSORY EXPLORATIONS allow young children to learn by using their senses. A large part of any study of the human body should include sensory explorations. Following is a sample of sensory activities (Webb, 1988).

Educators can set up a table of things to look at and provide equipment for children to use to get different visual effects. Hand lenses, prisms, binoculars, kaleidoscopes, and a plastic container of water to look through are a few suggestions. Children should be encouraged to use the tools to look at various objects and describe what they see.

Children can use their sense of touch to find and count pennies or pieces of macaroni "buried" in cornmeal or sand. They can identify letters, numerals, and geometric shapes while blindfolded.

Caregivers can fill small paper bags with dry ingredients such as flour, noodles, dry pet food, dry beans, and bird seed. They can prepare small plastic bags with the same ingredients inside. The children can reach into the plastic bags and, without peeking, match by feeling the ingredients in the paper bags.

To develop the sense of hearing, a teacher can help group of children tape record familiar school sounds and let their classmates identify the sounds. They can use a five to ten meter (five to ten yard) length of old garden hose and speak to each other through the hose.

A teacher might begin to read a book to the children while just moving his lips. After the children's reaction that they can't hear, the educator might discuss with the children the precious gift of hearing and how children must take care of their ears. The teacher or a guest might demonstrate sign language for the children.

Smelling and tasting are senses that complement each other. As children eat different foods, they should be encouraged to smell the foods first and talk about the tastes.

A teacher might cook rice for the children and let them taste and smell plain rice, buttered rice, salted rice, or rice with a bit of sugar and cinnamon. The children could taste various foods while holding their noses and see the effect that smelling has on taste.

An outdoor walk could be an opportunity for children to smell objects and to eat a snack out of doors.

OBSERVING ANIMALS is possible in any setting, and a variety of animals can be seen. Educators might take children outdoors and seat them for several minutes to watch and listen for signs of animal life. Do the children see or hear insects and birds? Can they detect evidence of other kinds of animals?

If the children are successful in noticing animals, the adult can write down some of the children's observations. Next, the children might explore the area for beetles, caterpillars, and worms on the ground. They might find spider webs, squirrel nests, and other signs of animals. The children might speculate about other kinds of animals that live in the neighborhood.

ANIMAL VISITORS in the classroom may be arranged by the teacher. A parent or other guest can bring any kind of tame animal for the children to see. The children should be seated. The guest can show the animal's features and talk about the care it needs. Perhaps the guest can feed the animal.

The teacher can help the children review the characteristics of living things and discuss the features the animal exhibited; perhaps the animal moved, reacted, and ate. The guest might talk about the animal's growth--what it looked like as a baby or will look like as an adult.

If it is safe to do so, the guest might let the children touch the animal. After the experience, the teacher can help the children write and illustrate a group composition.

ANIMALS HELP PEOPLE; PEOPLE HELP ANIMALS. People and animals share the planet Earth and are mutually dependent. Educators can talk with the children about animals that benefit from people's care, and the ways that people help animals. The children might scan magazines and books to find pictures that illustrate these ideas.

They could draw and classify pictures under the headings "Animals Help Us" and "We Help Animals." The children could set up a sharing table to display animal products and pictures of the relationship between animals and people.

ANIMAL HABITS AND HABITATS are amazingly diverse. To help children gain understanding of these ideas, educators must provide a rich variety of experiences and books. The classroom library should have books

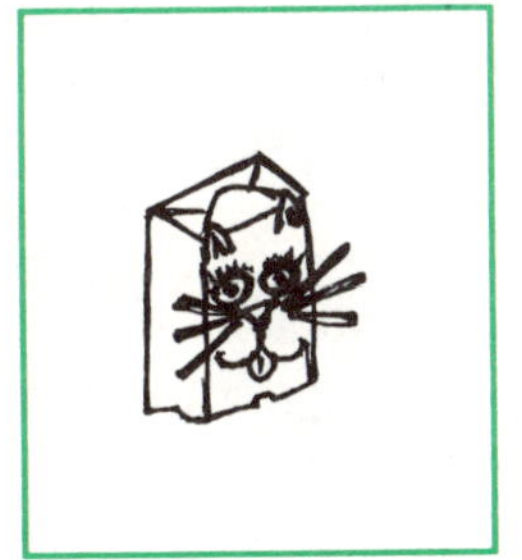

with photos and drawing of animals. The children should see as many live animals as possible.

The children can translate what they see and hear about in many ways. They can make clay and playdough models of animals. They can make habitat boxes showing little scenes of where animals live. The models and pictures the children draw can be placed in the boxes.

Wearing simple paper bag masks, the children might play the roles of animals. The class might make a big animal mural over a period of several days. The mural could include a background scene embellished with glued-on sticks, grasses, dirt, and sand. The children can draw and cut out animals to add to the scene.

PLANTS WE SEE. In any neighborhood children can see a variety of plants. The class might take a walk and see how many different plants they can see. The children can look for trees, bushes, grasses, ferns, vines, and other plants. Perhaps the children can gather several leaves or pieces of grass.

The adults can take notes as the group makes interesting finds. Back in the classroom the children can make a display of the specimens.

PLANTINGS GALORE. Children can grow plants in many different ways. As they do so, they learn that plants, as living things, grow and change. Plants need water, light, and something to grow in. Feelings of responsibility and pride are fostered as children grow plants.

Inexpensive and reliable seeds for children to plant include dry beans, popcorn, radishes, alfalfa, and mung beans (bean sprouts). Children can plant their seeds in plastic cups, on damp sponges and paper towels, in plastic bags with dirt or damp cotton in the bottom, or on a damp rag which will be rolled up.

The children should examine their plants each day and water them regularly. As the plants grow, the children can keep records of the growth in various ways.

They can draw pictures, use invented spelling to write narratives, or cut paper strips to the lengths of their plants and use the paper to make a bar graph.

Adults can help children begin to understand that plants are living things. They grow. They use water and sunlight to make food; plants derive some nourishment from minerals in the soil and from fertilizer. Plants respond to stimuli--they shrivel without water; many plants turn yellow without enough sunlight.

EXAMINE AN AREA. Educators can help children take a close look at some of the plants and animals around them. Children can work in groups and partition areas of the ground to examine. The children can fasten yarn around a square or circular area about a meter (one yard) across. They can sit down and look closely at the area noting all the different kinds of plant and animal life the area contains.

The area might also contain rocks, dirt, and things made by people. The children can compare two or more areas, discussing all the ways the areas are alike and different. They can classify some of the specimens found in the areas. They might group the specimens as green and not green or living and nonliving.

PLANT ART possibilities are also endless. The children can paint and print with leaves, sticks, and grasses. They can make crayon rubbings of flat plant specimens. They can press leaves and flowers and mount these between pieces of clear contact paper or  press-enclose them between waxed paper and seal them, under adult supervision, with a warm iron.

Children can make seed collages or paint with fingerpaint sprinkled with cornmeal or birdseed to add texture. Children can rub plants onto fine-grained sandpaper to leave different colors and effects.

Adults can boil plants like cranberries, onion skins, blueberries, and pecan shells in water, then help the children use these natural dyes to tie-dye tee shirts or paper towels.

After children have completed several art experiences using plants, adults might ask the children for more suggestions, then follow up on some of the children's ideas.

Science Activities Emphasizing Environmental Sciences

Earth and environmental studies help children become more aware of the world in which they live. Study of the earth's surface, what the surface includes, and the ways the surface changes are appropriate for young children.

The weather affects children' activities every day; science provides opportunities for children to learn more about it.

The universe has long fascinated people. Young children can begin to develop interests in space through study of the moon, stars, sun, and planets. They can begin to explore an exciting part of today's modern world--space travel.

DIRT 'N' ROCKS. Most people hardly notice the dirt and rocks around them, but a close look at these parts of our earth can be an involving activity for young children.

Educators can help children dig in the dirt with spoons and shovels. They can draw children's attention to the layers and colors of dirt the children will uncover. The children can feel the dirt and see if it is grainy (quartz-based) or smooth and slippery (clay-based).

 They can compare the smells of wet and dry dirt, sand, and other things they find. The children can feel the temperature of the dirt as they work with it; probably dirt near the surface will be closer to air temperature than dirt below the surface.

If children find rocks as they dig, teachers should encourage them to save the rocks to work with later. Teachers can also help children find and collect rocks at construction sites, in gravel driveways and roads, and in gutters. In areas where few rocks can be found, adults could supply some rocks gathered at other locations.

Some families may be able to share rocks and mineral specimens they have gathered at other locations. Children can wash and examine their rocks. Children might "shine" clean rocks by rubbing them with a bit of vegetable oil.

The children can hold their rocks and try to arrange some in order from heaviest to lightest. They can sort rocks into piles by size, color, texture, or whether rocks are shiny or not shiny.

Caregivers might help children to make "adobe" bricks by mixing wet dirt and grass clippings. The children can work in the mixture with their hands, then set their bricks in the sun to dry. The children might try to build an adobe structure with their bricks.

To increase children's hand-eye coordination, teachers can provide a bucket of rocks and some smaller plastic containers. The children can use tongs to move the rocks from the bucket to the smaller containers. Adults could mark levels on the containers with marker or with rubber bands and the children can fill the containers to levels that are full, half full, and so on.

WHICH ROCK IS IT? Children can play "I'm thinking of a rock." They can give clues, one at a time, to tell others which of several rocks they are thinking of. Adults can help children to give general clues such as "It's a big rock" or "It's hard," first, and then offer more specific clues, such as color or texture of the specific rock.

The children could also choose a rock and an adult could take dictation of all the descriptive words the children can think of that pertain to the rock. The rocks and descriptions can be displayed together.

OUR EARTH'S CHANGING SURFACE may be examined by children. After a rain, the children can look at places where water has flowed and left splash marks and tiny "stream beds." They can see how many puddles contain dirt and leaves that have been moved from their original loca-

tions.

The children might be able to find places where the wind has caused erosion. Adults can help children spot areas where people and machines have changed the surface of the earth. The class might take on a project to stop erosion by planting grass or other plants.

If children hear newscasts of tornados, floods, and earthquakes, educators should discuss these events and the problems that changes in the earth's surface cause people.

WEATHER AND SEASONAL DATA gathering should be a part of the usual classroom routine, especially during times when the weather might change in dramatic ways. Chapter 1 of the book presents ideas for gathering and sharing weather data on a daily basis.

To help children remember and understand changes over a longer period of time, caregivers might help them make a monthly weather poster. The children could write a few weather highlights on the poster each month. They could gather a few specimens (leaves, grasses) and tape them to the poster. If any dramatic weather events such as a violent storm or unexpected snowfall have occurred, the caregiver could help children make note of these things.

The children could display the weather posters and refer to them occasionally to review the year's weather. The children can also make seasonal collages. Adults can prepare large letters for the names of the seasons. Different groups of children can tape and glue specimens to represent the seasons to the letters. These can be displayed outside the classroom. After completing the letters for spring, the children might compare the ways they have collaged those letters to those they did for fall and winter.

WEATHER ART PROJECTS planned by creative educators can enhance weather phenomena for children. For example, children can paint with water colors, then hold their paintings in the rain for several seconds to make beautifully patterned rain paintings.

They can make wintry drawings with crayons, then paint over their papers with a strong solution of table salt or Epsom salt and water. When the pictures dry, the salt crystals will give a wonderful frosty effect.

Children can cut or tear paper shapes and tape these onto colored construction paper. The compositions can be taped to a sunny window and left for several days. The children can then take down their pictures and carefully remove the taped-on paper pieces; the sunlight will bleach part of the background paper and vivid designs will be left.

DRESSING FOR THE WEATHER is an everyday occurrence that makes children aware of weather effects. Teachers can encourage children to share and deepen their knowledge of weather and clothing by providing felt dolls and clothing of various kinds. The children can dress the dolls and talk about the occasions when clothing such as warm jackets, rain coats, boots, shorts, and hats would be appropriate.

Children can select clothing pictures from catalogs and magazines and glue these to paper. They can then draw a background to show appropriate weather conditions. Children can match pictures of clothing and weather conditions.

SKY GAZING offers many interesting sights. Children can see birds, planes, clouds, and the sun.

At night they can see the moon, stars, and planets, as well as planes and satellites.

After outdoor observations, children can draw pictures on light blue paper to portray things they saw in the sky. The children can note the position of the sun at various times of the day without looking directly at the sun.

An adult can help children use a prism to break sunlight into rainbow colors and describe those colors as they are cast on a white sheet of paper. The children can cast shadows in various shapes--long ones, short ones, fat and skinny ones, and even shadows with "holes" in them.

During the wintertime, educators can ask children to observe the night sky with their families in the early evening. Educators might suggest that families look at the moon and see its changing shape over a period of several days. They can also look for stars and planets. To follow up in the classroom, children can make nighttime pictures gluing bits of foil, white paper, and glitter to dark paper.

SPACE TRAVEL is accepted by today's young children as a normal part of life. Teachers can help children learn more about it by using pictures, videos, films, books, and newspaper pictures of space travel and space probes. After some background knowledge is presented, children can make models of space ships and space suits.

With a background of space music, they can pretend to walk on the moon or in space; children can move as they would in a weightless environment. Role playing about space can extend into the block center and dramatic play area. The children can transform a large box into a space ship. They can make space helmets and space suits from boxes, garbage bags, and plastic wrap.

Science Activities Emphasizing Physical Sciences

Study of physical science topics helps children see how things work. As they explore topics such as magnetism, water, light, air, machines and force, sound, and heat, children begin to better understand and appreciate the world. Understanding physical phenomena helps children be more aware of realities in the world. Children can also investigate how people use physical forces to help them in everyday life.

IDEAS FOR WATER PLAY have been presented in this chapter. Water play is attractive and relaxing for most children, but to sustain children's interest, educators can add many props to the water play area. Some additional ideas are given.

Sponges, funnels, clear plastic congeners and tubing, egg beaters, spoons, and plastic pitchers are a few suggestions. Adding food color or soap suds to the water gives it qualities that may be new and intriguing to children. When the weather is cool, adults can help children use warm water; in warm weather, adding some ice cubes will make the water even more inviting.

Educators can encourage children to experiment with objects that float and sink in water. After children test objects to see what the objects will do, they can sort the objects into two piles-- those that float and those that sink. The children might discover that some objects like lids float when they are carefully placed in the water, but sink when they are placed in the water on their sides.

WATER RACES are fun for children. They can work in teams and use various tools and utensils to transfer water from one bucket to another as quickly as possible. Children can carry water in ladles or spoons from one location to another moving quickly and carefully in a relay fashion. Teams of children can sit with adults and dictate as many uses for water as they can in a given time interval. After several minutes, they can exchange and compare answers.

STATES OF WATER, depending on its temperature, may include liquid, ice, or vapor (steam). Teachers can provide ice cubes and have children discuss how long it will take the cubes to melt in different parts of the room. The children might speculate on means of preventing the ice from melting and try out some of their ideas.

As the children prepare recipes that use hot water, the teacher can have the children observe the steam. They might carefully catch some steam on a cool metal or mirror surface and see the steam condense into liquid form.

EXPERIENCES WITH HOT AND COLD WATER occur daily. Children feel water of different temperatures as they consume drinks and wash their hands. Educators might also let children wash doll clothes in hot and cold water, then hang the clothes to dry.

An adult might help children dissolve flavored gelatin in hot water to prepare a dessert or use cold water to prepare a soft drink mix for the class. Children can try to dissolve salt or sugar in hot and cold water. They will probably find that solids dissolve faster in hot water than in cold water.

Children can watch closely as a drop or two of food coloring is placed in a glass of hot water and in a glass of cold water. The food coloring blends and mixes more rapidly in hot water than in cold.

Solutions the children mix can be poured into styrofoam trays and set aside for several days. The children might predict what will happen to their solutions, then check on them each day and describe the results.

AIR IS REAL. Children can feel the effects of moving air as they run and feel the wind against their faces or watch the breeze move the leaves and branches of trees. They can use plastic bags to capture air. If they seal the bags, then press against them, children can feel the "push" or pressure of air. When children release bags of air they can again feel the coolness and movement of air.

Children can force lots of air into balloons by blowing hard into the balloons. If children release their balloons, the balloons fly around the room as air leaves the bags with enough force to propel the balloons.

Children can sweep large plastic bags through the air, then use twist ties to close the bags tightly. They can draw on the bags to make large air-filled creatures.

Children can make little boats with triangular bases cut from styrofoam. They can attach sails to their boats with toothpick masts. The children can float their boats in water and blow on the boats or fan them to make air to move the boats. Adults can encourage the children to use words such as faster, slower, closer, and farther as they describe the boats' movements.

Children can examine and think about many foods and classify the foods as to whether they contain much air or not. Foods, like popped corn, whipped topping, bread and biscuits are "fluffy" and have small visible air spaces. Foods like un-popped corn, fruits, or butter have fewer visible air spaces.

Teachers can discuss with children the fact that people need clean air to breathe. They can lead the children in taking long deep breathes and shorter panting breaths.

The children can sit quietly outdoors and count the breaths they take in a period of thirty seconds. The children can then run and jump for several minutes, then count their breaths again. Most will find that exercise causes the body to use more air as people burn food for energy; thus the breath rate becomes faster.

Teachers can help children examine pictures of people skin diving or photos of astronauts. The children can find and discuss the devices that help people to breathe in these conditions.

PROPERTIES OF LIGHT are observable. Light helps people see. To make this fact real to children, caregivers can seat the children, then make the classroom as dark as possible. They can encourage the children to describe what they can (and can't) see. The caregivers can then use a flashlight or candle and carry it around shining it on various objects--near one child's face, near another child's shoes, on a table, and so on. The children can see how light makes things easier to see.

After this experience the children could draw pictures of well-lit and dimly-lit scenes. Children can look inside a large box and see how it is dark inside; they can help to cut a window and see how it is easier to see when light can enter the box.

Children can peek through paper towel tubes or 1-2 meter (1-2 yard) lengths of old hose. They can discover that when they line up the tube of hose with a light source, they can see the light. When the tube and light are not lined up, The children won't see the light source; light travels in straight lines.

MAGNETS OFFER FUN AND LEARNING. They are fascinating objects for children to manipulate. Children will discover that when pairs of magnets are held in some position, they "stick together" or attract; in other positions, magnets "push apart" or repel each other.

Magnets attract some metal objects--those made of iron, steel, nickel, and cobalt--but do not attract other metals. A teacher might gather many small objects for the children to test with magnets. She can attach several bits of a strip magnet to a steel file cabinet. Children can make predictions about whether the objects will attract to the bits of magnets or not.

The children can take turns trying out the objects. Those that attract will stay on the filing cabinet surface; those that don't attract will fall to the floor. The children can gather other objects and test them to see if they attract to the magnets.

Children might bring magnets from home and share a variety of magnets in different sizes and shapes. They can test the magnets to see if that are all the same strength or not. The children can compare the number of paper clips each magnets will attract. They could make a chart of their findings.

Magnets attract through various materials such as paper, wood, water, and air. If paper clips are placed on top of a piece of poster board, children can hold a magnet under the posterboard and move the paper clips.

Children could make a little stage from a cracker box. They can make little puppets from paper, spools, or paper cups and attach thumbtacks or paper clips to the puppets. The children can manipulate the puppets with a magnet held under the box.

The children can make styrofoam boats and attach paper clips to the boats. The boats can also be moved by a magnet held above the boats or under a pan of water.

VIBRATIONS CAUSE SOUNDS. An adult can have children watch as he stretches and plucks on a rubber band. The children will hear a sound and see the vibrations. Children can work in pairs and hold rubber bands for each other to pluck on. They can describe the movements of the rubber bands and imitate these movements with their bodies. The children might sing as they "vibrate," then on a signal from the caregiver, stop singing and moving at the same time.

Each child can hold a hand over his throat as he talks and sings and feel the vibrations of the vocal chords. As children sing high notes, they can notice that their voice boxes are high in the throat; with lower tones, the voice box falls to a lower position.

The children can observe other vibrating objects and the noises they make. For example, they might place rice on the lid of an empty coffee can. They can see that when the can is struck, it make a small sound and the rice jumps and vibrates.

Perhaps an adult or older child can demonstrate the playing of a string or brass instrument; the children can hear the sound and gently feel the vibrating parts of the instrument. The children can draw pictures of their experiences with sound and vibrations.

MACHINES HELP PEOPLE move things and perform work. Teachers can have children assemble all the wheeled vehicles and devices they can find in the classroom The children can examine the wheels and see how the wheels spin smoothly.

They can push a toy car on its wheels and then on its top and notice that the vehicle moves with less effort on its wheels. The children can lift a large stack of books, then push the stack along the floor and notice the force that is necessary to move the books. They can then move the books on a wheeled cart and see that less force is required to move them.

The children could look around their homes and find examples of wheeled devices. At school the class could compile a long list of things with wheels that people use to help them.

The children can look around the classroom to find other examples of tools and machines that help people. They might try to sharpen a pencil with their hands, then see how much easier a pencil sharpener with its wedge-shaped blades makes the work.

The teacher could let the children try to crack nuts with their hands, then with a nut cracker to see another example of a tool that lets people apply force and do work more easily. The children could go on a neighborhood walk and look for examples of machines and tools. Each child could draw one or more examples of tools for a class book.

Science: Every Day, Everywhere

Science is everywhere. Science is an area that is appealing to young children and one in which they can become deeply involved if they are given opportunities. To help children learn more about themselves and the world, educators must plan and implement a variety of science activities for children.

Chapter 6

People Working Together for Young Children

Children represent the future of our country and world. Adults must find ways to educate children as effectively as possible to enrich children's lives and also to prepare them as future citizens and workers. An important task for today's educators is to find ways of working together on behalf of children and better educational opportunities for children.

This chapter will present some ways that educators can work together to help children. They can work together as colleagues planning appropriate experiences and policies for children. Educators can also work with parents and members of the community to secure support and help for the important job of educating children.

Colleagues Working Together

Often educators work in collaboration. Collaboration means shared decision making or problem solving. Hall (1988) describes some advantages of collaboration. Collaboration is uniquely task-centered. People emerge from collaboration with a feeling that they have helped to shape future events; they have a feeling of "ownership" when decisions are made jointly.

Collaboration helps people gain a clearer sense of what is to be done and how to go about doing it. As a result of the give and take that is inherent in collaboration, people feel satisfied that the most important considerations of a situation have been explored.

Collaboration has even more benefits (Hall, 1988). In situations where people collaborate on ideas for benefitting everyone and being more productive, satisfaction and commitment are greater than in situations where people do not collaborate. Feelings of responsibility and pride are enhanced. Frustration is decreased. Thus, there are many benefits to collaborating.

At the New Horizons Educational Summit (1988) leaders described education as a life-long learning process. They state that in traditional learning, individual and competitive efforts are emphasized. A life-long learning model places value, however, on cooperative and collaborative efforts.

Rather than teachers being implementors of curriculum, the life-long learning leaders described teachers as professional decision-makers; thus, teachers should work toward collaborative planning and learning.

Hall states that collaboration is an invitation to share power. Teacher empowerment is much discussed in education. Peterson (1990) describes empowerment as active involvement of teachers in decision-making. Teacher work together to make and implement plans on matters that concern them.

Dillon (1990) states that empowered people are high- energy people who know themselves and what they want to achieve. They are ready to accept responsibility and need new challenges. Whitlock (1990) adds that empowered teachers make good decisions based on sound knowledge of people and policies. They influence what happens in their schools as well as in their classrooms.

Mitsoff (1990) reminds us that empowered teachers are lifelong learners. They consider actions in light of their philosophies and based on understanding of the way that children learn.

The importance of teacher decision making and empowerment is highlighted by Maeroff (1988): "The teacher is the basis of schooling...the input of teachers must give shape to the forming of education; it cannot be left to others to make all the important decisions. Knowledgeable teachers who act as professionals can improve the education of their students." (p. xiii).

The characteristics of empowered teachers described by these authors fit those of many early childhood educators. They hold strong convictions about ways of helping young children to develop and of assisting families to better understand their children.

Early childhood educators are social, caring persons who enjoy working together and sharing ideas. They are usually receptive to learning new techniques and information; they are in the business of learning and helping children to learn.

Educators and caregivers interested in collaboration and the empowerment that it provides might meet and brainstorm some of the matters on which they could collaborate. Planning units and unit themes is one area that directly affects children; ways of planning units were presented in the first chapter of this book.

Educators can also plan or revise their system of dealing with discipline, communicating with parents and families, utilizing local resources, and arranging for professional and personal development.

Educators and caregivers might want to study the philosophy that their educational agency espouses. If no statement of philosophy or mission exists, educators should develop one.

Existing statements of philosophy and mission should be reviewed periodically to see if the statements are current and appropriate to serve the needs of children and their families and staff. In discussing policies and procedures, collaborators will want to see how well their plans or suggested actions complement their philosophy.

LEADERS AND PARTNERS. In collaborative situations people act as leaders, but also act as partners as they work together toward the same goals. As people assume leadership roles, they often have or develop characteristics that distinguish them from others.

Some of the leadership characteristics described by Gardner (1990) are that leaders are able to think in the long terms--beyond the current day's activities or problems--and that leaders are able to think about their units and the larger constituencies they serve.

For example, a kindergarten teacher may help others think about goals for an entire year. She may be able to think of discipline policies in terms of benefits to many children, not just the child who is very challenging at the moment. Such a teacher may be able to see her role in preparing children for future schooling, but also to be effective family and community members.

Gardner states that leaders put heavy emphasis on "the intangibles of vision, values, and motivation..." and have the social skills to resolve conflict. They are kind, diplomatic, and able to communicate with different groups of people. Leaders also think in terms of renewal and seek to revise "process and structure required by ever-changing reality." (p.4). In other words, leaders are receptive to change.

Gardner describes even more attributes of leaders. One essential attribute is physical stamina, vitality, or physical durability. Even after a day with children, a leader is likely to be able to suggest fresh ideas at a meeting or is anxious to plan creatively for coming events.

Leaders exhibit intelligence and judgment in action. The can combine hard data, questionable data, and intuitive guesses to arrive at conclusions and at future courses of action.

Leaders exhibit willingness to accept responsibility. They exercise initiative. There is much to be done in early childhood education; thus, there are many chances for different people to assume positions of leadership. Many leaders seem to need to achieve; they are driven by strong inner forces to work on behalf of others.

Leaders also exhibit task competence; they have knowledge of the tasks at hand or are willing to find and develop the knowledge and skills necessary to accomplish things.

Leaders also have social skills. They understand and appreciate the needs and motivations of others and are thus able to move others to action, "to communicate persuasively, to strengthen confidence" (Gardner, p. 51).

Leaders have courage, resolution, and steadfastness. This gives them the confidence to approach a school board, board of directors, or legislator on behalf of children and their families.

Often leaders have the capacity to win and hold the trust of others. This characteristic may be due, in part, to the confidence leaders have in themselves. This capacity is valuable in working with children, parents, and administrators.

Finally, Gardner's list of attributes of leaders includes organizational abilities. Leaders are decisive. They decide on priorities and get things done. Yet leaders are also flexible in their approaches. If one tactic is not efficient or effective, leaders will find other ways of reaching their goals and achieving the results that will help children and their families.

Virtually every early childhood educator acts as a leader at some time. The profession appeals to some because of opportunities for leadership that it offers. Whether it is leading a group of children, trying a new approach and being knowledgeable and enthusiastic enough to make it succeed, sharing ideas with colleagues, or acting as hostess on parent's night, educators assume leadership positions.

Knowledge of leadership characteristics and attributes helps educators reflect on strategies to play their roles in effecting change.

Educators also act as partners and followers as they work together, attend professional meetings, and participate in community and professional group work. Effective followers or partners listen well, make suggestions, and lend moral support to their leaders. They do their parts in working to support decisions made by their leaders or groups.

COLLABORATIVE PLANNING. Collaboration has many advantages. It is facilitated when individuals work together as leaders and partners. What other conditions are necessary for effective collaboration? Hall (1988) suggests that administrative support is one basic need.

Administrators must be willing to share power and decision-making with well-informed teachers and caregivers. Administrators must show that they value contributions from their workers and give feedback on suggestions that teachers and caregivers make. Administrators must provide a flow of information to their workers.

Calkins (1986) suggests that the initiation for collaborative efforts must come from teachers or co-workers rather from administrators; when collaboration is mandated "from above," often, it is resented.

Nevertheless, administrators can facilitate collaboration by supporting staff-initiated efforts. For instance, administrators can provide a place for teachers to meet and meet with the teachers when requested to do so. Administrators could provide refreshments for meetings.

Perhaps they could facilitate a plan for teachers and their assistants to meet during the children's rest time with minimal staff staying with the children.

Calkins also writes about leadership in collaborative groups. Most collaborators want a leader or facilitator to initiate discussions and guide directions. When the leader is a peer, she need not be an "expert" who knows all the answers. Some groups establish rituals to help them make the best use of their time and to increase their productivity.

One group might begin meetings by sharing recent learnings and successes. In another group, the members might begin with few minutes of making notes about their concerns and sharing these with others.

Working with Parents and the Community

The authors of **Education: A LIfe-Long Learning Process** (1988) suggest that parent involvement in education is essential. Educators should see parents as partners in the education of children.

Parents have intimate knowledge of children. Naturally, they are concerned with children's long-term growth and progress. Their perspectives and support can help educators know children better and therefore work with more sensitivity and insight.

Ball (1985) points out the wealth of information that parents and other family members can share with educators. If educators are aware of stresses, needs, and expectations of families, they can better plan for children.

They also gain insights into the kinds of communications and involvement that parents would find helpful and valuable. Galinsky (1988) adds that until educators have information about parental needs and problems, they cannot consider realistic goals for children.

Becher (1986) reports that substantive evidence shows that parental involvement in children's education promotes both academic achievement and cognitive competence. Educational involvement also enhances parent-child relationships.

Another effect of parent-school cooperation is that parents become better "teachers" at home and use more positive means of discipline with their children than parents of children who are uninvolved with the school. Involved parents are also more positive about schools and school personnel; often they help to garner community support for educational programs.

With all the possible benefits of parental involvement, some educators are still reluctant to encourage it. Why? Becher (1986) states that teachers are sometimes uncertain about how to involve parents and still maintain their roles as "experts."

They question whether planning for parental involvement will take too much time. Parents also sometimes complain that the bureaucracy of schools discourages involvement and their expression of concerns, complaints, and demands.

Many of these problems can be overcome if educators reach out to parents and work to build a feeling of trust and open communication. Becher states that successful family involvement programs employ several principles.

They realistically consider the time and skills that the staff can devote to family involvement efforts. They respond to parent schedules with creative and flexible program activities. They involve parents in decision-making and explain administrative decisions; thus, parents are encouraged to respond to decisions rationally. They expect problems but emphasize solutions. Because problems are anticipated, procedures for resolving them are developed and communicated to parents. "Failures" are not blamed on parents.

Approaches to Parent Involvement

Ways of involving parents and other members of children's families vary widely. Some schools and day care programs encourage parents and family members to visit the educational setting to observe or act as volunteers. They hold parent meetings, open houses, and parent teacher conferences. Others provide written information to children's families to inform them of happenings at school and the children's progress.

PARENTS AS HELPERS IN THE CLASSROOM. Parents can perform a variety of tasks and offer other support in the classroom. Volunteer parents might read to individual children, or listen as children "read" to them. They might supervise children in the block center or dramatic play area or help a group of children at a learning center.

Parents can assist with routine chores such as

filing examples of children's work in their cumulative folders, cleaning up in the art center or after snack, or helping to arrange the room for rest time. On neighborhood walks or field trips, parents are always welcome to help with supervision and conversation.

Parents can conduct special activities in the classroom. Perhaps a parent could help a group of children prepare an ethnic recipe and share the results with the rest of the class. Perhaps the parent could teach the children a special song, dance, or poem. A parent may be willing to lead the children in exercises or outdoor physical activities.

If parents serve regularly as volunteers, educators will want to provide some orientation. Parents should know where supplies are kept and should have a roster of the children's names. They will profit from a brief explanation of the teacher's approach to learning activities and from specific instructions on what they are to do each day. Some educators write explanations of activities on note-cards for their own use; these cards can easily be shared with the parent who is conducting an activity.

PARENT CONFERENCES When educators and parents or guardians meet face-to-face to communicate, many helpful understandings and outcomes can emerge. In some schools educators try to meet with each child's family member at regular intervals to describe the child's progress and to gain the parent's insights on the growth of the child.

In other situations educators see parents as problems arise. Though the former approach is more time-consuming, it has several benefits. Educators keep in touch with each family and build a base of support for each child as well as for the school. Parents are not threatened by being called to school only when problem situations have developed; this makes many parents feel more comfortable.

To make conferences productive, educators might write a letter to parents alerting them to things they might want to think about and discuss. Parents might list questions or topics they have for the teacher. Educators should welcome parents with a handshake, a smile, and friendly words.

Conferences should take place in a comfortable quiet area. Educators might want to seat themselves beside family members rather than across a table from them. Educators should try to start conferences on time, and stay with a schedule. If problems remain unresolved or if family members want to converse more, they can be invited to schedule another conference rather than keeping the next family waiting.

Educators should start and end conferences with positive words. They might show parents examples of the children's work or a checklist of observations of the child's behaviors. Some educators make audio- or videotapes of the children and offer to lend the tapes to families to play at home. Educators might have ready suggestions of things families can do at home to complement and supplement the school program.

When educators have specific problems to discuss, the problems should be described fairly and objectively. Parents should have a time to comment. Galinsky (1988) outlines six steps to a problem solving process with family members.

The first step is to identify and describe the problem while avoiding accusations or implying that the source of the problem is with the personality of the child or parent. The parent and educator should next generate several possible solutions to the problem and discuss the strengths and weaknesses of each suggestion. They should come to a consensus of which solution to try and discuss how to implement it.

Finally the educator and family member should agree to meet again and evaluate how well the chosen solution is working. If changes in approach are needed, these should be discussed and initiated.

Occasionally, parents are in need of health services, family counseling, or other special services beyond the scope of normal school activities. Educators might compile a list of resources and resource people for family members to contact. A school administrator or counselor might coordinate such information to supplement what the teacher is able to provide.

FAMILY MEMBERS AS RESOURCE PEOPLE. Children's family members can be interesting resource people who can share their knowledge and talents. Not only can classroom visitors interest and inform children, but a child feels a special pride when a family member visits his class.

Family members can share information about their jobs. Factory workers might show products they make or demonstrate special tools they use. Medical workers--from dental technicians to nurses aides to physicians--can talk about ways they help people and ways people can stay healthy.

Medical workers and others might wear their special uniforms and show the children features such as pockets, name badges, special shoes, and headgear. Mechanics might show children their tools and talk about the ways that machines work.

People who provide services--hair stylists, store clerks, or government workers--will have special skills to demonstrate. Educators can follow up any visit by letting the children draw and write about the visitor, by letting children write thank-you notes, and by setting up a complementary dramatic play situation.

Hobbyists and collectors can share their collections, special tools, and skills. A skin-diver might wear her wet suit and show the children her breathing gear and underwater photos. A retired person could show the children how she knits, crochets, or sews. An artist might draw a sketch or work for a period of time in the classroom. Other guests might demonstrate archery, dog training or grooming, playing an instrument, or wood carving.

The South abounds with agricultural resources. Family members can help the children learn more about farm and forestry products. A farmer might visit at harvest time and show soybeans, cotton, or vegetables. A tree farmer could show "baby trees" and describe the importance of forest lands for providing wood products, adding to a healthy atmosphere, and preventing erosion.

A catfish farmer might show a small catfish and describe what the fish eats and how it is cared for. A livestock farmer with any baby animal is sure to make an impression on the children. A fisherman could show some of his equipment and the creatures that he catches.

Visits from children's older siblings or young adult relatives are very exciting and informative. Junior high or high school athletes might show their equipment, demonstrate training procedures, and talk about healthy lifestyles.

Older students who are community volunteers might tell the children what they do and why they like their jobs. Fast food workers might visit the class in uniform and show some of the products that they sell and serve. Young military personnel could also visit the class in uniform and tell how they serve their country. They might teach the children to stand at attention and salute and present some special "military vocabulary."

NEWSLETTERS Many individual educators and schools use regular newsletters as a way of communicating with parents. Educators who want to initiate a newsletter should make several decisions: To whom will the newsletter be sent? Will it be sent by mail or taken home by children? The latter approach is inexpensive.

When a child regularly lives with two parents in a divided family, some educators send the newsletter home to the parent with whom the child is staying and mails a newsletter to the other parent.

How long will the newsletter be? When will it be produced? One newsletter per season or per month is reasonable frequency in many circumstances. Will the newsletter have a name and logo? If so, it will be more recognizable to families.

If a substantial number of parents speak and read languages other than English, educators should make efforts to provide newsletters in languages the families can read. The reading level of the newsletter should be appropriate for its audience.

Educators will also want to decide if the newsletter will have regular features like reports on the activities of each classroom, a column from the principal or director, or a feature of things that parents could do with their children at home.

If the newsletter will have these features, educators should decide who will be responsible for writing them and when copy will be due.

Who will produce the newsletter? It might be typed by the school secretary and printed on the copy machine. Perhaps a teacher or two will add artwork and illustrations. Costs for a simple newsletter are minimal, but a local business or industry could pay for its production. Educators should be sure to acknowledge and thank any sponsors for their support.

What will the newsletter look like? It might be reproduced on standard pages with or without columns. Standard or legal sized paper could be folded to make a booklet format.

Colored paper is attractive and will help make the newsletter seem attractive and special. Children's artwork, perhaps reduced in size on a copy machine, can be added for appeal and to recognize the value of children's art.

Newsletters usually feature what the children are learning and provide descriptions of the processes they use as they learn. If special events have occurred or special people (including family members) have made contributions to the school, the items should be emphasized.

As often as possible, children's names should be mentioned. Some newsletters include lists of the children's birthdays. A class group composition could be included, especially if it has "quotes" from all of the children. Parents often appreciate previews of upcoming events so they will be aware of what will be happening in the near future. Newsletters can include lists of things--styrofoam trays, spools, sewing scraps, and so on--that families can collect and share with the school.

Parent education articles will be welcomed. Parents and other family members might learn from descriptions of the values of activities that seem like "just play."

For example, educators might describe some

of the things children learn as they work with blocks, water, or sand. Educators could describe how and why the class writes group compositions or how the children use "invented spelling." Before a holiday parents might welcome suggestions of appropriate toys and gifts to buy for their children.

CALENDARS. Educators can compile monthly calendars for parents and families. The calendars could include notices about special dates for families to be aware of. They can include briefly-written descriptions of activities families can do at home to develop communication skills, cognitive skills, and adult-child bonds.

Calendars can be sent home with newsletters or separately. Some educators leave spaces for children to draw on and decorate the calendars before they take them home. Calendars are particularly valuable to keep in touch with children who are not in school in the summer.

A July newsletter might feature a variety of items for the Fourth of July and for warm weather use. Some of the descriptions of activities could extend across more than one date. Little sketches could fill any empty spaces.

The calendar might begin with general instructions such as: "This calendar suggests ways of keeping learning 'alive and well' during the month of July. We hope you will complete all of the activities with your child."

Descriptions of specific learning activities might include:

Talk to your child about all the shapes you can find in the U.S. flag.

Discuss family plans and traditions for the Fourth of July. Involve your child in cooking a special food for the holiday.

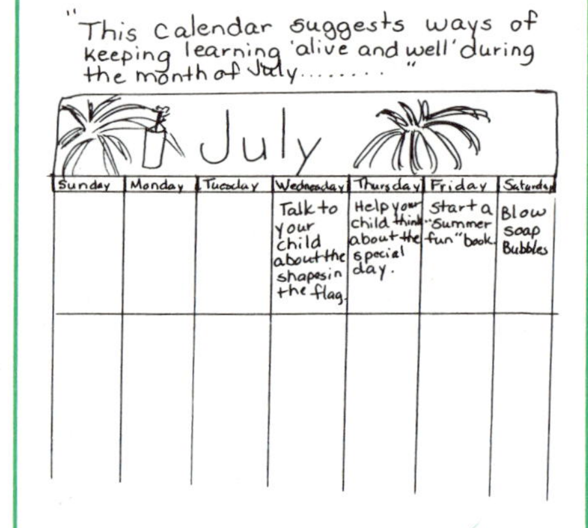

Talk about reasons we're lucky to live in the United States.

Help your child think back about the Fourth of July holiday and choose a favorite event. Talk about why it was fun or meaningful.

Talk to your child about things that are red, white, or blue. Make a list and add to it for several days.

Start a booklet of "Summer Fun." Have your child design a cover and write a page or two. (On subsequent days, make suggestions of things for the child to add to the book.)

Add things to your child's water play area. Sponges, plastic tubes, cups, and bottles will be fun to use. Add ice cubes or soap suds too.

Other suggestions for a July calendar might include blowing soap bubbles, counting the days until school reopens, taking a walk to find and discuss flowers, and making a collage of summery items.

OPEN HOUSES. Open houses or receptions in the classroom give families a chance to visit the school in a group. They provide opportunities for educators to display children's work, chat informally with parents, and present a brief program.

Educators might set out materials in learning centers and display cards telling the purpose of the materials and the processes children use as they work with the materials. Educators might invite parents to use the materials.

Educators could take slides of children, being sure that each child is included in a picture or two. The slides can then be worked into a brief informative slide show telling about happenings in the classroom. Photos displayed on a bulletin board can provide similar information.

Experience charts and books made by the children should be displayed and mentioned at the open house. A sample of the children's art work can be displayed.

If the weather permits, an outdoor art show is attractive and encourages family members to move about and converse. Perhaps folders of each child's work could be made available to family members. Large paper figures (tracings of each child's body) can be colored and displayed in the classroom.

Children can help to prepare simple refreshments for the open house. Recipe charts the children used can be displayed. If children are invited to the open house, they can help to serve the refreshments and clean up. The children can decorate placemats to use with the refreshments.

Today's parents have busy and demanding schedules. Educators should give careful thought to scheduling open houses so that as many families as possible can attend. Evening meetings are a possibility, especially if children are invited. Some schools ask parents to drop in for an open house as they pick up their children in the afternoon. Even an early morning open house might fit the schedules of some groups of parents.

HONORING FAMILY MEMBERS. Many times during the year children can show appreciation for family members. At Thanksgiving children can give thanks for their family members and the support they provide. At Christmas or Hanukkah children can make gifts for family members. On Valentine's Day children can prepare cards for their families. At Mother's Day and Father's Day, children can honor their parents or other special persons.

Because children's family structures and lifestyles vary, educators must be sensitive to the fact that not all the children have the same family members or relationships. To help children recognize and accept a variety of family structures, educators can discuss the ideas that some families are headed by single parents, stepparents, grandparents or other relatives, or foster parents.

The educators can encourage children to tell about their own family structures. Adults can stress the idea that no matter what the family structure, family members love and try to support and help each other.

To make the children more aware of their helping roles in their families, educators might help the children prepare three experience charts. The children can dictate ideas for "Things I help with in my family," "Things family members help me with," and "Things I do by myself."

The children might compose one chart each day and on the fourth day review their ideas and add to the charts. Educators can share the children's ideas with their families in a newsletter or at an open house.

Children can cut pictures from catalogs, magazines and newspapers to show things they would like to give their family members. These can be presented as "gifts." Children can also make little "coupon books" of promises to do household chores or make others feel good. The children can make small pictures for these books and staple the pages together.

Cards to family member are always welcome. Making cards gives children a chance to be creative and to express themselves with pictures and words. Five- and six-year old children can put their cards in envelopes and write addresses on them.

Even if the children "hand deliver" their cards, practice in writing addresses will be profitable.

Most parents and special family members will value children's art work when it is prepared as a gift. Educators can help children make cardboard and paper frames for drawings and paintings; parents will appreciate the date placed on art work.

Children can make large tissue paper flowers as gifts. They can cut out several petals and leaves and wind a pipecleaner around them. The teacher can help the children fasten the petals with tape or staples and fan out the petals to make attractive fluffy flowers.

Children can grow real flowers and plants to give as gifts. These need to be started well in advance. The caregiver should grow several extra plants in case some of the children's plants do not grow well. Children can also make dried or pressed flower arrangements for their families.

A Final Word

The time educators and caregivers spend working together and working with members of children's families is time well spent. People can collaborate to generate ideas and alternatives to help children learn and grow.

Working together lets people be creative and collegial. They feel a sense of power and fellowship as they communicate and take action on behalf of children. They feel pride in themselves and the work they are doing. What better use of time and energy is there than working together on behalf of happy, healthy, capable children?

References

Anderson, H.O. (1989). Board establishes the new NSTA Division of Multicultural Science Education. *NSTA Reports!,* November, 1-3.

Ball, R.A. (1985).Ideas! Parent involvement: How and why. *Dimensions,* 14 (1), 15 - 18.

Becher, R. (1986). ERIC Digest: Parents and schools. *ERIC Clearinghouse on Elementary and Early Childhood Education,* OERI # 40-83-0021.

Berk, L.E. (1985). Research in review: Why young children talk to themselves. *Young Children,* 40, 46-52.

Brooks, L.H. (1986). "A study of the effects of systematic listening instruction on the reading comprehension achievement of first grade students." Unpublished field study, University of Mississippi.

Calkins, L. (1989). Personal sharing: Supporting each other. *Learning,* 16 (4), 84.

Cazden, C.B. (1981). **Language in early childhood education,** revised edition. Washington, D.C.: National Association for the Education of Young Children.

Charlesworth, R., and Miller, N.L. (1985). Social studies and basic skills in the early childhood classroom. *The Social Studies,* 16, 34 - 37.

Cliatt, M.J.P. and Shaw, J.M. (1988). The storytime exchange: Ways to enhance it. *Childhood Education, 64,* 293-298.

Day, B. (1988). **Early childhood education: Creative learning activities.** New York: Macmillan.

Dillon, D. (1990). Untitled selection in Pinning down empowerment, *Instructor,* January, 26 -28.

Feeney, S., Christiansen, D., and Moravik, E. (1987). **Who am I in the lives of children?; An introduction to teaching young children.** Columbus, OH: Merrill.

Galinsky, E. (1988). Teachers and caregivers: Sources of tension, sources of support. *Young Children,* 46 (3), 4-12.

Gardner, J. (1990). **On leadership.** New York: Free Press.

Goffin, S., and Tull, C.Q. (1988). Encouraging cooperative behavior among young children. *Dimensions,* 16 (4), 15-18.

Graves, D. (1983). **Writing: Teachers and children at work.** Exeter, NH: Heinemann.

Hague, K. (1986). **Numbears.** New York: Henry Holt.

Hall, J. (1988). **The competence connection: A blueprint for excellence.** Woodlands, TX: Woodstead Press.

Hoban, T. (1972). **Circles, Triangles, and Squares.** New York: Macmillan.

International Reading Association. (1986). Joint statement on literacy development and pre-first grade. *The Reading Teacher,* 39, 819 -21.

Jackson, K. (1982) **Dinosaurs.** Washington, DC: National Wildlife Association.

Leigh, L.M. (1990) Collaboration: Benefits and challenges. *Early Childhood Leadership News,* 3 (3), 10 - 11.

Leigh, L.M. (1986). *A whole language approach to writing and thinking.* Jackson MS: Mississippi State Department of Education.

Leigh, L.M. (1988) Research and practice: Young children's writing. *Early Childhood Leadership News.* 3 (3), 1-7.

Maeroff, G.I. (1988). **The empowerment of teachers.** New York: Teachers College Press.

McClelland, S. (1989) Every child a poet. *Early Childhood Leadership News.* 4 (4), 13-17

Mitsoff, K. (1990). Untitled selection in Pinning down empowerment. *Instructor,* January, 33.

Morrison. G. (1984). **Early childhood education today.** Columbus, OH: Merrill.

National Council for the Social Studies. (1981). Essentials of the social studies. *Social Education,* 45, 162-164.

National Council for the Social Studies. (1984). In search of a scope and sequence for social studies. *Social Education,* 48, 249-262.

National Council of Teachers of Mathematics. (1989) **Curriculum and evaluation standards for school mathematics.** Reston, Va.:NCTM.

National Science Teachers Association. (1987). **Criteria for excellence.** Washington, DC., NSTA.

New Horizons Educational Summit. (1988). "Education: A life-long learning process." Paper of the Project/ Models Team.

Penick, J. E., and Yager, R. E. (1983). The search for excellence in science education. *Phi Delta Kappan,* 9, 621 - 623.

Peterson, D. (1990). Untitled selection in Pinning down empowerment. *Instructor,* January, 28-29.

Ranger Rick's dinosaur book. (1984). Washington, DC: National Wildlife Association.

Tatum, J. (1988). Journals in the kindergarten. *Early Childhood Leadership News,* 3 (3), 8-9.

Templeton, S. (1986). **Family Literacy.** Exeter, NH: Heinamann.

Torrance, E.P. (1972). "What reseach says to the teacher: Creativity in the classroom." Washington, DC.: National Education Association.

Trelease, J. (1985). **The read aloud handbook,** revised edition. New York: Penguin Books.

Webb, T. M. (1988). Research into practice: Sensory development. *Early Childhood Leadership News,* 3 (4), 12-15.

Whitlock, J. (1990). Untitled selection on Pinning down empowerment. *Instructor,* January, 28-29.